Love, Across All Languages: A Global Journey

By

Jotham Ndanyuzwe

LOVE, ACROSS ALL LANGUAGES
A GLOBAL JOURNEY

Published by Jotham Ndanyuzwe, Edmonton, Canada

Cover design by: PageMaster Publishing

Cover photo by: Flux Media YEG

Paperback ISBN: 978-1-77354-547-9

eBook ISBN: 978-1-77354-550-9

Publication assistance and digital printing in Canada by

PageMaster
PUBLISHING
PageMasterPublishing.ca

Dedication

I want to thank my family and friends for their unwavering support in allowing me to attain my goals.

I want to thank my loving wife, Benisse Ndanyuzwe, for his everlasting support and patience, which have provided a solid basis for my life. Your faith in my skills has worked as a spark for my growth through difficult situations, encouraging me to set lofty objectives.

With the help of Pastor Emmanuel Rwagasore's counsel and knowledge, I have a clear grasp of my path and am motivated to continue on it. Your encouragement has stayed significant during difficult times, providing support and inspiration.

Pleasant Ndatabaye's presence as a companion has greatly impacted my general well-being and emotional comfort. I am appreciative of the tremendous contribution you have made in translating difficult chores into entertaining group activities. Your influence has been astounding, and I will be eternally grateful.

I want to offer my heartfelt appreciation to Theogene Umbwiyeneza for her considerable help and persistent support. I genuinely appreciate your degree of faith in me, as well as our friendship.

Sarah Bink, I appreciate your offering of fresh viewpoints and ideas. I am grateful for your devotion and work in contributing to this discussion.

I want to thank Theogene Umbwiyeneza for all of her assistance and support. Your unfailing belief in my skills has been a constant source of encouragement, and I am grateful for your company.

Sarah Bink, your insightful insights and distinct points of view have substantially increased the breadth and depth of my work. The contributions have been beneficial, and I am grateful for the insightful feedback.

Acknowledgments

I want to convey my gratitude to all who have made major contributions to the successful completion of this project.

Benisse, your everlasting tolerance, deep understanding, and unselfish sacrifices have served as the basis upon which my successes have been built. The user expresses thanks for the inspiration and motivation supplied by the user's unwavering belief in their abilities and potential.

I want to convey my appreciation to Theogene Umbwiyeneza, whose unrelenting dedication and unrivaled assistance were critical to the successful completion of our project. I am grateful for the tremendous support offered since the suggestions and contributions supplied have substantially increased the project's worth.

I want to thank Ghostwriters Hub for their amazing support and skill throughout the writing process. I appreciate your attention and work in aiding me in expressing and transferring my ideas into a written form. Your input has been really helpful in making my ideas come to life.

I want to thank Ghostwriters Hub for their amazing support and skill throughout the writing process. I appreciate your attention and work in aiding me in expressing and transferring my ideas into a written form. Your input has been really helpful in making my ideas come to life.

About the Author

The author, Jotham Ndanyuzwe, entered the world in South Kivu, DRC, in 1994. He moved to Rwanda when he was ten and finished elementary and secondary schooling there. After relocating to Nairobi, Kenya in 2014, he continued his theology education at the Canadian school known as World Impact Bible College (WIBI). There, he completed the requirements for a diploma in Christian ministry. Therefore, Jotham relocated to Canada in 2019 to study Forensic Science at the prestigious Stratford Career Institute (SCI).

Jotham has shown a deep passion for missionary activity that parallels his dedication to education. While in Kenya, he was instrumental in evangelization and establishing new churches. Before leaving for Canada, he was ordained as a pastor in Nairobi, where he had played a key role in forming Good News Announcers.

Jotham, who currently lives in Canada, is an active member of the Steele Heights Baptist Church there. On February 27, 2021, Jotham Ndanyuzwe added to his list of accomplishments by beginning a new chapter by marrying Benisse Ndanyuzwe.

Chapter 1: Introduction

In this chapter, we step away from the languages and cultures that are known to us in order to focus on the strength that may be found in love. We investigate the role that love plays in fostering peaceful coexistence among people of varying racial and ethnic backgrounds, as well as religious and national convictions. It is brought to our attention that love has the power to create new connections within communities as well as to strengthen the ones that currently exist. We shed light on the universality of this powerful feeling by looking at how love may bridge linguistic, cultural, and societal boundaries. Specifically, we look at how love may cross the language barrier.

The transformational power of love, both on an individual and a cultural level, is another topic that will be covered in this chapter. We look at how love can bring people together and shine a light on difficult circumstances, all while inspiring compassion, sympathy, and empathy in those who experience it. In order to highlight the relevance of love in the process of developing and maintaining good relationships, we investigate the effect that love has on people's feelings of contentment, joy, and overall sense of accomplishment.

As we continue on our voyage across the world and begin to investigate the different facets of love, we lay the foundation for followlng chapters in the book. The following pages will unveil the language of love and its potential to transcend all barriers, both linguistically and culturally, through the use of illuminating anecdotes, a range of points of view, and sound advice. This will be accomplished by examining the language of love through the lens of its ability to cross all boundaries. We are going to investigate the ways in which love may bring about positive change in both individuals and the wider world.

It is fascinating to think about the ways in which love may bring about positive change, lessen suffering, and restore relationships. Love's unique capacity to stir up empathy and comprehension is what makes it so effective at bringing individuals closer together. This is the secret of love's popularity. As we go further into these victories of love, we gain a deeper understanding of the power that love possesses to bring about change.

We will also discuss the complex relationship that exists between romantic love and an individual's sense of well-being and contentment in their own lives. Love has a significant influence on the happiness and joy that we experience in our own lives. When we both give and receive love, we strengthen our connections with other people, as well as our sense of self-worth and our sense of belonging to a community. Love, in all its guises, has the power to transform our identities and the decisions we make, therefore allowing it to enhance the quality of our lives.

Let's go off on our adventure around the world with our minds and emotions completely open to the possibility of falling in love.Learn how the concepts that lay behind this lovely feeling, love, have the potential to overcome all barriers to communication and understanding. The following stories and teachings are designed to help you really examine the power of love to change people, establish connections, and leave a legacy of goodwill and peace in the world.

Throughout the course of this book, we will learn about some very remarkable people and organizations that have used the transformative power of love to make the world a better place. These stories, which emphasize acts of generosity and sacrifice that create relationships as well as adventurous, romantic initiatives that defy social expectations, will serve as a monument to the enduring power of love since they highlight acts that forge relationships, such as acts of kindness and sacrifice that forge relationships.

In addition to this, we will talk about the difficulties that couples experience while attempting to overcome prejudice and cultural barriers. We are going to have a conversation about how cultivating compassion, tolerance, and open-mindedness may help persons from all walks of life appreciate and respect one another more deeply. By cultivating these characteristics, we might make the climate more favorable for the growth of love and for the reconciliation of our disagreements.

We will also talk about the importance of commitment, honest communication, and forgiveness in maintaining healthy and successful relationships. We'll see firsthand how love and forgiveness can mend broken hearts, reignite lost faith in one another, and forge more meaningful ties between people.

We will also examine the ways in which technology has altered love relationships and discuss the challenges and opportunities that come with trying to keep the spark alive in today's world of constant connectivity. We will discuss the significance of setting reasonable limits online, maintaining open channels of communication, and cultivating trust with online acquaintances.

Throughout the course of our trip, we're going to stress how important it is to love and care for oneself first in order to have successful relationships with other people. We are going to talk about how you may improve the quality of your life as well as the relationships you have with other people by creating strong boundaries and having a positive opinion of yourself.

We are going to ponder our recent life-changing experience and reflect on what we have discovered and learned as a result of it. In order to pass on a legacy of love, compassion, and understanding, we will strongly encourage you to incorporate the lessons and stories that we will share with you into your own life and the relationships that you have.

Let's go on this love adventure together, which will take us overseas across continents and language barriers. By the use of shared experiences and narratives, we may get an understanding of the enormous potential of love to have an effect not just on our own lives but also on society as a whole. Through an exploration of the many facets of love, we hope to encourage and make it possible for individuals to form relationships that are more congenial, mutually helpful, and respectful of one another and the world as a whole.

As we make our way through the complexities of its worldwide journey, we will also investigate the significant influence that love has on personal development and reflection. Love has the capacity to bring forth our authentic selves, motivating us to expose our vulnerabilities, confront our phobias, and develop as unique individuals. We will investigate the ways in which love and relationships may help us become our best selves, as well as the ways in which partnerships can help us become better versions of ourselves.

During the course of our travels, we are going to get a deeper understanding of the complicated relationships of parental love, passionate love, and platonic friendship. We will talk at detail about every conceivable kind of relationship, as well as the difficulties and opportunities that come along with each one. We'll see how love, in all its guises, can mold and improve our lives, from the first kiss of a new relationship to the unwavering loyalty of parents and the strong links of friendship. This will be an eye-opening experience for all of us.

While we are traveling, we will be forced to confront the ways in which society and cultural standards influence romantic relationships. In an effort to encourage readers to embrace love in all of its manifestations, regardless of cultural norms, we will challenge traditional narratives and look for new points of view. This will be done in an effort to persuade readers to accept love. If we did this, it would be possible for us to make a contribution toward the growth of a society that values and respects all different kinds of interpersonal interactions.

We hope that as readers make their way through the stories and experiences described in this book, they will pause for a moment to consider their own connections with others and the things they have picked up along the way. Through introspection and contemplation, we may gain a better understanding of our own requirements, desires, and emotional capacities. Because we have a better awareness of ourselves, we have a better chance of establishing connections with other people that are sincere, courteous, and emotionally profound.

We have high hopes that the observations, suggestions, and activities included in each chapter will serve as a foundation for the readers as they begin on their own amorous and intellectual adventures. We have high hopes that the material will pique the readers' interest and cause them to reflect on how it could be relevant to their own lives and the people they care about. This will cause waves of compassion and comprehension that will extend far beyond the confines of these pages.

The book "Love, Across All Languages: A Global Journey" concludes with a challenge to see love as a unifying force that may dissolve boundaries and create relationships based on mutual respect and understanding. This is a call to action at the end of the book. We believe that a deeper knowledge of the power of love and a devotion to that power might contribute to the creation of a world that is more peaceful, interdependent, and free of language and borders. Therefore, let's go out on this adventure together and see what all the fuss is about when it comes to love.

The power of love has not just a profoundly favorable influence on romantic relationships, but also on friendships, family bonds, community ties, and other types of interactions. The ability of members of a family to care for and support one another is founded, first and foremost, on love. It increases feelings of trust, empathy, and open communication by fostering a sense of belonging and safety in the community. The emotional support and the provision of a secure environment for honest communication that is provided by the love that is shared within families is beneficial to the development and well-being of individuals.

Love is a force that brings people together because it enables people to set aside their differences and work together for the sake of the community. People who love one another are more prone to look out for each other, which in turn cultivates feelings of compassion, empathy, and respect for one another.

When people feel like they belong and are linked to one another, the social fabric becomes stronger, and people are more likely to support and encourage one another.

Love has a significant influence not just on personal connections but also on families, communities, and other types of interactions. It is possible that this will have a beneficial domino effect that will boost the mood of everyone who is a member of these groupings. Realizing one's full potential as a human being as well as feeling like they belong and having a purpose in life are fostered through cultivating and fostering love within families and communities.

Love shared among families and communities helps to provide a foundation for a support network that enables individuals to triumph over obstacles and take part in the pleasures of life. It fosters harmony and cooperation, both of which are beneficial to the surrounding community. In addition to being a powerful motivator for people to work toward bettering themselves and the communities in which they live, love also encourages people to make positive contributions to the wellbeing of those in their immediate environment.

Love is an essential component in the process of establishing strong connections among various social groupings, such as families and communities. It promotes members of the family to communicate with one another in a way that is both open and understanding. Love helps to cultivate unity, compassion, and mutual respect, all of which contribute to the formation of social relationships and an improvement in the well-being of society. If we want to construct a society in which every citizen has the opportunity to flourish and can count on the support of their fellow citizens over the course of their life's journey, we must begin by cultivating love within our own families and communities.

It is impossible to overestimate the role of love in the process of constructing healthy connections both inside individuals and between individuals, families, and communities. People are able to be themselves in the safe environment that is created by it, talk about their experiences (both good and sad), and look to others for solace and direction while they are doing so. When there is love in a family, everyone experiences what it is like to be welcomed and treasured for who they are.

Love has a ripple effect that can be felt by those who are not directly related to the object of that affection and can extend out into the wider society. A community that is filled with love makes its members feel a greater feeling of togetherness, understanding, and responsibility for the whole group. It encourages individuals to reach out to one another and help, particularly when circumstances are difficult. Through acts of compassion, caring, and assisting one another, love strengthens the social fabric of the community and gives individuals the sense that they belong to one another and the community as a whole.

The love that exists between families and communities is another powerful source of motivation and inspiration. When people have the sense that they are loved by their family, friends, and the people in their community, it inspires them to develop and improve themselves as individuals. Love is the engine that propels positive transformation. It provides people with the fortitude to push through challenges, pursue their ambitions, and contribute positively to their families and communities.

Additionally, love has an influence on families and communities that can be felt for many years to come and even across generations. Parents and other adults in the community create an environment that is loving, which serves as a model for younger members of the community. They learn the significance of being kind, courteous, and understanding as a result of this. The act of loving one another evolves into a custom that is carried on from one generation to the next. This results in the formation of loving and supportive relationships that go on to develop further.

In a nutshell, love is an essential component in the process of constructing healthy connections within families and organizations. It creates a secure environment in which individuals may develop by giving them the sense that they belong, that they are welcomed, and that they have support. When there is love in a community, it inspires individuals to treat one another with kindness and to assist one another when they are in need. Not only do we make the connections that we currently have stronger, but we also create the way for a society that is more compassionate, welcoming, and peaceful when we allow love to blossom in our families and communities and encourage its spread.

It is actually remarkable how love has the power to draw individuals together, enhancing their capacity to care for and comprehend one another along the way. Love has the power to see past differences and tear down barriers, allowing individuals to experience a deeper sense of connection and oneness with each other. When we make room in our hearts for love, we allow ourselves to become more receptive to the ideas, emotions, and experiences of other people.

Love is the only force capable of tearing down the barriers that prejudice and judgment create. This enables us to see under the surface of our differences and recognize the common humanity we all possess. It helps us cultivate a profound feeling of compassion and understanding by instilling in us the value of treating other people with the courtesy and respect they deserve. Love teaches us to pay attention to what other people are saying, to validate and acknowledge the emotions and experiences of others, and to appreciate the unique qualities that distinguish one person from another.

When we let love into our hearts and minds, we are better able to empathize with people and comprehend their experiences. Because of this, bridging barriers and connecting with others in meaningful ways is made much simpler. Love compels us to consider the world from the perspective of another person and to extend a helping hand. It compels us to put ourselves in the position of the other person. As we seek to alleviate the suffering of people around us and lift their spirits, it inspires us to be compassionate, giving, and unselfish in our actions.

Love also gives us a sense of belonging and serves as a constant reminder that we are all interconnected and dependent on one another. It opens our eyes to the fact that our own wellbeing is inextricably linked to that of others and that we have a responsibility to look out for one another's interests. Love compels us to acknowledge the things that we share in common with others and to rejoice in the qualities that set us apart. This contributes to the development of an open and accepting society.

Love, in the end, possesses the potential to transform not just individuals but also entire communities. It has the power to heal wounds, bring people together, and inspire individuals to collaborate in order to create a society that is more compassionate and understanding. By making love our guiding principle in how we interact with one another, we may create a society in which compassion, empathy, and comprehension are the norms, as well as a world in which the bonds that bind individuals to one another are strengthened. This will result in a better and more peaceful future in the future.

In addition to bringing people closer together and making them more compassionate and understanding of one another, love is an essential component in ensuring that individuals within families and communities have meaningful connections with one another. Love gives people a sense that they belong to a group and draws individuals closer together. This creates an environment that is supportive and compassionate, one in which individuals have the opportunity to develop and succeed.

Love is the foundation of healthy and enduring relationships within a family. People are provided with a secure environment in which they are able to be themselves and in which they will be welcomed for who they are. People who are loved in their families are better able to deal with adversity, feel better about themselves, and form bonds that are more likely to endure. It encourages open communication, empathy, and mutual respect among family members, all of which contribute to the family's ability to work through challenges together and improve as a whole.

People are brought together by love in a way that transcends their differences and provides them with a sense of having a common goal in life. Love draws individuals together and increases the likelihood that they will cooperate with one another and care about the well-being of others. It inspires others to want to be kind, giving, and helpful, which initiates a chain reaction of good things that extends well beyond the scope of individual connections.

The presence of love in a community makes its members feel more connected to one another and serves as a constant reminder that we are all interconnected components of a larger whole. It encourages people to consider the well-being of others rather of focusing solely on their own requirements and preferences. By engaging in acts of love and kindness, communities have the ability to combat social inequality, advance justice, and create environments in which everyone is made to feel appreciated and supported.

Love among families and communities may also serve as an inspiring model for future generations. When a child is shown love and compassion throughout their formative years, it teaches them the importance of characteristics such as empathy, understanding, and acceptance. They are more likely to have relationships that are healthy and compassionate throughout their lives and to pass on these values to future generations, so establishing a legacy of love that extends well beyond the current moment.

In this chapter, we'll discuss how love may have a significant impact on not just households but also entire communities. We will examine the ways in which love may transform relationships, facilitate better understanding among individuals, and give them a sense that they are a part of a community via the use of illuminating anecdotes and practical pointers. We are going to get an understanding of how love may transform not just our lives but also the world around us, leaving behind a legacy of compassion, harmony, and contentment.

Love has a significant impact on a person's overall feelings of contentment, fulfillment, and physical well-being. The presence of love in our life, whether it be romantic love, love between members of the same family, or love between those we hold most dear, bestows upon us a profound feeling of joy and contentment.

Love gives us the sense that our lives have purpose and that we belong somewhere in this world. When we have the sense that we are loved and connected to other people, we get the perception that our lives have greater significance. Love provides us with a justification for caring, for putting effort into our relationships, and for assisting and supporting one another. It provides us with a cause to live and the opportunity to participate in something that is more significant than ourselves.

Love is also beneficial to our emotional and psychological well-being. It provides us with a sense of security, trust, and mental support, all of which assist us in coping with the challenges and uncertainties of life. When we share our ideas, feelings, and shortcomings with someone we love, we don't have to worry about being judged or rejected because love provides us with a safe space to do so. This mental and emotional fortification comes about as a result of receiving emotional support and validation, both of which contribute to our overall sense of well being.

Additionally, love makes us happier and increases our overall level of happiness. Our hearts feel pleasant and warm when we are aware that we are loved and cared for by others. Love is responsible for bringing about periods of happiness and ecstasy, in addition to a sense of comfort and tranquility. It enhances our happiness, makes us feel better overall, and provides us with a positive outlook on life.

Love encourages people to develop and become the best versions of themselves. When someone loves us, they want us to be authentic versions of ourselves, to pursue our unique passions and abilities, and to realize the aspirations we have for ourselves. Love paves the way for personal development by providing an environment in which we are able to learn and develop with the assistance of people who love and support us.

Love has an influence on our level of happiness that extends well beyond the connections we have with other people and into a great many other aspects of our life. When we have the sense that we are loved and supported, we are more inclined to engage in activities that bring us joy and make us feel good about who we are as individuals. When we're in love, it makes us want to pursue the things that we're passionate about. It inspires us to explore new territories and expand the scope of our perspectives. It gives us the confidence to step outside of our comfort zones and put our efforts toward maturing and developing as individuals.

Because it improves our mood and lowers our levels of stress, love plays a crucial role in the maintenance of our overall health. When we are in love, our brains produce hormones like oxytocin and serotonin, which make us feel joyful, relaxed, and healthy in general. When we are not in love, our brains do not produce these chemicals. These biological reactions not only help us feel better, but they also contribute to the maintenance and improvement of our physical health. They can, for instance, strengthen our immune system and reduce the likelihood that we will develop chronic diseases.

The feeling of mental peace and safety that people experience as a result of love is another benefit. When we know that we are cared for by another person, regardless of the circumstances, we have a greater feeling of safety and security. This mental support functions as a buffer against the challenges and uncertainties of life, decreasing people's levels of stress and helping them feel better overall. Love helps us get through challenging situations by providing us with strength, understanding, and someone on whom we can depend.

Not only does love effect how happy and content we feel, but it also influences how we feel about ourselves and how much value we place on ourselves. When other people love us, it acts as reassurance that we are excellent, and it also assists us in maintaining a positive picture of ourselves. Love helps us find our strengths, recognize our unique talents, and accept ourselves as we are. Both the development of a positive perception of oneself and the maintenance of physical well-being depend on the cultivation of feelings of love and acceptance toward oneself.

Additionally, love inspires us to prioritize our own needs and to take good care of ourselves. When we love ourselves, we understand how critical it is to attend to all aspects of our wellbeing, including our physical, mental, and emotional states. We take care of ourselves by engaging in activities such as physical activity, maintaining a healthy diet, focusing on the here and now, and practicing various kinds of relaxation. These routines contribute to our overall pleasure and feeling of well-being because they help us take care of both our bodies and our minds.

Love has an impact on our well-being and the degree to which we feel our lives are complete that extends beyond the confines of our individual lives and into the realm of the community and society as a whole. We contribute to making the world a friendlier and more peaceful place when we strive for the creation of a society based on love and kindness. Acts of love and kindness have a multiplier effect, inspiring others to want to participate as well and setting in motion a chain reaction of positive occurrences. Love has the power to transform not just our own lives but also the people we associate with and the communities in which we reside.

Love's positive effects on a person's life satisfaction, happiness, and overall well-being have a ripple effect on that person's mental, psychological, and even physical health. A caring companion may improve a person's disposition, level of contentment, and quality of life.

A great feeling of emotional stability, acceptance, and belonging are gifts that come to us from love. It is a place where no one can judge us or make us feel terrible for being who we are, and we can do the same for them. When we are loved, folks around us care about us, listen to our words, and respect our feelings. They will also take the time to listen to what we have to say. When we share the ups and downs of life with another person, we feel a more profound sense of emotional connection and a greater understanding of accomplishment.

Love is a powerful force when it comes to our sense of who we are and how much we are worth. When we realize that other people love, cherish, and appreciate us, it significantly impacts our sense of who we are as individuals. Love teaches us to value our unique qualities, look past our flaws, and consider the possibility that we deserve love and happiness in our lives. When we have a healthy perspective on who we are, we are better equipped to face the challenges that life throws at us and come out on the other side with hope and determination.

Love tremendously impacts many facets of our well-being, including the physical health of those who experience it. It has been shown that those with healthy connections report lower stress, anxiety, and depressive symptoms than those who do not have healthy relationships. The feeling of love triggers the production of feel-good neurochemicals in the brain, such as endorphins and oxytocin. These compounds contribute to overall well-being and may even have physiological effects, such as lowering blood pressure and improving immune function. Loving relationships benefit your health for several reasons, including the fact that they provide a sense of belonging and emotional stability.

Love is a powerful motivator for personal development and progress. When we believe that our efforts are appreciated, we have the confidence to work for our objectives and realize our full potential. When we have feelings of care and concern for another person, we want to do all in our power to earn that person's affection and respect. It inspires us to confront our phobias, venture into the world, and grow as individuals.

The effects of love extend far beyond a single person, permeating not just our interpersonal connections but also the social fabric as a whole and impacting both. It is possible to acquire the qualities of love, such as empathy, compassion, and understanding, via education. It promotes more open and honest conversation, careful listening, and an easy willingness to forgive, all of which lead to better and more meaningful relationships. Love also motivates us to provide a helping hand to other people and perform kind acts for others who are not directly linked to us in some way. It is possible to develop communities that value love and compassion by promoting these ideals within those communities.

In the end, love is a potent energy that has a significant impact on the levels of happiness, fulfillment, and overall health that we experience in our lives. It not only makes us happier but also brings us together with other people, improves our mental health, and contributes to our overall growth as individuals. Love fosters behaviors such as self-acceptance, self-care, and self-nurturing, all of which contribute to a more positive perception of oneself as well as increased levels of self-esteem. Its impacts are not limited to individual relationships but extend to the community as well as to society as a whole. We have the opportunity to create a world that is kinder, more peaceful, and more gratifying for everyone if we are willing to accept love and share its spirit with one another.

Chapter 2: Love Knows No Boundaries

I'm amazed by how love can unite people regardless of ethnicity, religion, or nationality as I learn more about this. Any type of bias or discrimination is invisible to pure love. It can bring people from all walks of life together and deepen their understanding of one another.

I have witnessed how love transforms individuals, even when it defies societal norms and expectations. I've seen how individuals from all backgrounds can connect and form enduring relationships via the language of love. It demonstrates how love overcomes financial and cultural barriers to embrace our shared humanity.

Through these relationships, I've witnessed firsthand how great it can be when individuals from all backgrounds come together to create something unique. They respect one another's differences as a basis for constructing a stronger culture. Because of their shared love, they dispel misconceptions and pave the way for more acceptance and tolerance in the world.

Prejudice may be destroyed through love that crosses racial, cultural, and national borders. It motivates us to converse with people who are fundamentally unlike us to deepen our worldview. It forces us to reflect on our biases and stereotypes, which in turn aids us in understanding the importance of diversity.

In a society that could seem divided, love turns into a vehicle for transformation and development. It inspires us to extend our perspectives and perceive the world as more interconnected and hospitable. Love teaches us that the commonalities we have with one another much outweigh any differences, and it inspires us to work toward establishing a culture that appreciates and respects every individual.

I'm hopeful when I consider the power of love to unite people. There are no boundaries to the power of love when I consider how it may bring us together despite our differences. It inspires us to recognize our shared humanity and the benefits of valuing our differences to create a more peaceful and harmonious society.

The brave people who defied common opinion and fell in love with someone of a different race, religion, or culture will be profiled in the following chapters. We may better comprehend the immense impact that love can have on an individual and society at large by learning about their experiences. Let's embark on an expedition and discover everything there is to know about the ability of love to bring people from all over the world together in friendship and understanding.

Here, we look at accounts of people from many walks of life making risky romantic gestures to show how love can overcome obstacles and inspire others to take chances. These stories are wonderful examples of how the pursuit of love can push people to go against their limitations, social norms, and cultural expectations.

There are examples of people who defied convention and acted on their convictions, even if, at the time, it may have appeared impossible given their ethnicity, race, or place of birth. These stories show the courage and tenacity of those who dared to defy expectations to pursue their passions.

As we hear the stories of interracial couples who overcome prejudice and discrimination and of those who pursued long-distance relationships across continents, people's remarkable propensities to dedicate themselves to love are on full show. These tales show the breadth and depth of their love for one another and how consistently they have accepted diversity and formed relationships with individuals from many walks of life.

These accounts offer insight into the courage required to overcome the challenges of love across cultural and societal boundaries. People are conquering their worries and those of their families, communities, and themselves to follow their hearts and discover boundless love.

The transforming power of love in conquering bigotry and prejudice is also seen in these examples. By sharing their experiences and questioning social norms, these courageous individuals are paving the way for more acceptance, tolerance, and empathy.

These narratives from actual experiences ultimately function as a poignant reminder that love transcends all limitations. These experiences prompt individuals to reflect upon their biases and foster an inclination toward embracing the myriad of perspectives and cultural variations that arise from developing affection for individuals from dissimilar backgrounds. These heartwarming narratives serve as a poignant reminder of the profound capacity of love to dismantle barriers, foster connections, and pave the way for a future characterized by greater equity and tranquility for all individuals.

Within this framework, we pay tribute to the fortitude and bravery exhibited by individuals who have embarked upon remarkable romantic endeavors, defying established conventions to embrace love that surpasses conventional boundaries. The narratives provided by these individuals illustrate the significant influence of love in eliminating prejudice, promoting cognitive and emotional development, and inspiring individuals to demonstrate acts of bravery and selflessness. The reader is encouraged to engage in introspection regarding their viewpoints on love and the limitless possibilities that emerge when embracing the inherent diversity within these narratives.

The study's overarching goal is to learn more about the human experience of coming to terms with the universality of love and its capacity to unite individuals of different racial, religious, and cultural origins. This research explores the hypothesis that love might operate as a uniting force, facilitating relationships that go against the grain of conventional wisdom.

Stories of individuals who defied social norms and improved society by pursuing romantic partnerships despite the risks involved are inspiring. The tales are a clever way to drive home that true love has nothing to do with conformity or deviation. Humanity's boundless potential is displayed in the unyielding fortitude and dedication shown by individuals who embrace love without conditions.

Two examples of the types of experiences included in this study are interracial couples who have surmounted prejudice and the personal voyages of individuals who have traversed vast geographical and cultural divides. These stories eloquently demonstrate the limitless potential of love. The protagonist's determination to surmount obstacles and establish meaningful connections moves and inspires the audience. The stories of these individuals illustrate how fortitude and compassion can help people confront and surmount life's inevitable challenges.

The misconceptions surrounding the transformative potential of love can be dispelled through open dialogue and the exchange of personal experiences. Love has the potential to break down barriers, broaden perceptions, and foster an environment where individuals from diverse backgrounds can learn to respect and value one another. These stories illustrate how people develop and evolve, inspiring us to maximize opportunities.

These individuals' bravery compels us to evaluate our own biases and preconceptions. People must examine the limitations they have placed on their ability to experience love and be receptive to the possibility of relationships that extend beyond those boundaries. The stories of these people have a big impact on our ability to understand and feel pity for others. They also make us think about how social rules limit love relationships.

This chapter examines how and why love can easily unite people from different races, cultures, and places. Those who have put themselves out there for relationships should be commended.

The experiences of these individuals inspire us, making us aware of and appreciative of the vast diversity of human connections in our society. They share anecdotes to illustrate how love can break down barriers between people of diverse backgrounds and cultures.

Knowing more about these heroic individuals makes us rethink our prejudices and presumptions. We are encouraged to embrace the limitless possibilities of love and pursue it as it leads us to self-actualization and fulfilling relationships. We go on a journey transcending cultural, racial, and national barriers because we are firmly convinced that love can change lives and knows no boundaries.

As soon as two individuals fall in love, they go on a journey to become used to and learn about one another's cultures. It demands a mindset open to understanding and empathizing with other people's traditions. By developing an openness to learning about and respecting other people's traditions, customs, and beliefs, couples may learn from one another. This discussion not only solidifies their relationship but also broadens their horizons in terms of thoughts and viewpoints.

When two individuals develop romantic feelings for each other, it is often observed that, despite their contrasting backgrounds, they can establish a meaningful connection. Individuals encounter various obstacles and cultivate benevolence, forbearance, and adaptability. In a mutually beneficial partnership, individuals in a healthy relationship actively seek opportunities to augment each other's attributes while maintaining their own distinct identities.

Recognizing the imperative nature of expending effort and fostering mutual comprehension to overcome cultural disparities is paramount. To foster success in a multiethnic relationship, it is imperative for partners to engage in introspection regarding their own biases and preconceived notions while also actively questioning prevailing cultural norms. As interpersonal familiarity deepens, individuals appreciate each other's divergent attributes and begin to acknowledge the diverse range of their shared cultural legacies.

Couples are additionally driven by affection to establish a societal framework that acknowledges and appreciates the disparities within their cultural legacies. Through establishing connections with various organizations, acquaintances, and mentors who have effectively addressed cross-cultural challenges, couples can receive support, comprehension, and companionship from individuals with prior experience in this domain. In these groups, couples can discuss the various challenges and successes experienced within their relationships while also receiving guidance from individuals with firsthand experience in similar situations.

The capacity to perceive divergences as assets rather than drawbacks is ultimately a consequence of a couple's mutual trust in each other. It fosters a sense of appreciation among children for the unique historical backgrounds that contribute to the depth of their relationships. By cultivating an environment characterized by mutual regard, comprehension, and curiosity regarding one another's cultural heritage, individuals can foster a unique amalgamation that symbolizes affection and commitment within the relationship.

Acknowledging their value is the first and most important step in resolving cultural differences. When partners invest time in understanding and valuing one another's distinctive experiences and viewpoints, respect and understanding may grow. Two people are more likely to consider their differences in cultural background as advantages to explore and cherish when they are truly in love.

We illustrate the transformative power of love across cultures via real-life examples of people from various backgrounds making risky romantic attempts. These couples transcend stereotypes and traditional knowledge by accepting and loving one another despite their differences.

When two individuals are in love with one another, they develop a strong bond. It fosters trustworthy interactions by creating a setting where both parties may express their thoughts without worrying about the consequences. Couples can transcend the linguistic and cultural obstacles that separate them by carefully listening to and attempting to understand one another.

But it's crucial to understand that navigating cultural differences can be challenging. Married couples frequently differ on issues like shared values and cultural standards. Couples in love have the fortitude to face problems head-on, cultivating an atmosphere of tolerance, compromise, and receptivity to new ideas.

Couples who believe in the transformative power of love can embrace their differences and deepen their bond. By being familiar with and partaking in one another's traditions, they may appreciate one another's distinct histories and connect through shared experiences.

Couples in love are also more likely to seek out local relationship specialists like mentors, counselors, and support groups. Couples can utilize this material to connect with others who have had similar circumstances and have their questions addressed. Through these programs, couples trying to improve their relationships of love and respect may learn from one another and find support.

We invite couples to share their ideas and perceptions regarding overcoming cultural barriers in their relationships in this area. We intend to support you in developing a devoted connection that honors each of your distinct cultural traditions. The purpose of demonstrating the transformative power of love in shattering cultural barriers is to inspire couples to embrace their differences, cherish their shared love, and create a partnership that embodies the richness of their intercultural experience.

Love transcends all barriers, including cultural ones. It acts as a motivating factor, encouraging couples to commit to a lifetime of knowledge and progress. Couples may create a relationship that not only survives the difficulties of cultural differences but also thrives in the rich tapestry of their shared experiences by creating a love that respects and loves diversity.

Understanding and acceptance are essential in a relationship between people from different cultures. Couples with varied cultural backgrounds aim to comprehend and share their emotions and experiences when they approach each other with empathy. Couples can forge closer ties and a greater sense of humanity by learning to put themselves in their partners' shoes.

Tolerance, however, entails appreciating the distinctiveness of various cultural experiences. The ability to tolerate variations in opinions, beliefs, and cultural customs without imposing one's own or insisting that others alter their behavior. Couples may exercise tolerance and create a safe space where both partners feel welcomed and accepted for who they are instead of feeling pressured to comply with a specific cultural ideal.

A relationship that exhibits mutual sympathy and acceptance between both spouses is more equipped to navigate the difficulties arising from cultural disparities. Individuals tend to adopt a more empathetic and compassionate approach when encountering disagreements, prioritizing constructive dialogue over rigid perspectives. Partners who possess empathic qualities exhibit enhanced comprehension and establish a robust emotional bond due to their heightened ability to empathetically understand and relate to the experiences and perspectives of one another.

Empathetic and tolerant relationships possess a greater capacity to recognize and value the unique contributions that arise from each partner's cultural background. Couples are encouraged to actively engage in each other's cultures and traditions to cultivate an environment characterized by mutual respect and intellectual curiosity. When couples develop an appreciation for and hold in high regard their unique characteristics, they have the potential to establish a robust and dynamic relationship founded upon a love that surpasses cultural limitations.

The levels of tolerance and empathy exhibited by the couple have implications for their relationship dynamics and interpersonal interactions. Couples from diverse cultural backgrounds who exhibit kindness and acceptance towards each other serve as exemplars for societal observation. Their primary objective is eliminating bias and exclusionary practices within their communities and the broader society. The mutual affection and admiration for each other's cultural legacies can exemplify a society that strives to be more embracing and diverse.

Tolerance and empathy are essential components in fostering cross-cultural connections. These establishments allow couples to cultivate romantic relationships and establish explicit guidelines rooted in mutual respect and fondness. Couples who actively engage in efforts to comprehend and nurture each other's needs and concerns foster the growth and development of their relationships and make valuable contributions toward establishing a more equitable and harmonious global society.

Empathy is a powerful tool for navigating the complexities of relationships marked by cultural differences. Regardless of an individual's cultural background, the ability to understand and empathize with the emotional state of one's romantic partner is a fundamental element. By fostering a deep emotional bond and nurturing empathetic comprehension, couples possess the capacity to augment and strengthen their interpersonal attachment.

When couples demonstrate empathy towards each other, they exhibit a state of attentiveness, engage in a reciprocal inquiry regarding each other's experiences, and actively endeavor to enhance their support and understanding of one another. Couples who actively practice empathetic listening exhibit a genuine desire to comprehend and affirm one another's emotions and individual experiences, cultivating heightened trust and intimacy in their relationships. Couples can cultivate an elevated comprehension and reverence for one another by embracing their partner's cultural standpoint, thus enabling them to perceive the world through their partner's cultural lens.

Tolerance and empathy are complementary attributes that contribute to cultivating an inclusive and accepting atmosphere. Cultural differences are recognized and valued without any bias or assumption of homogeneity. Couples have the potential to establish an environment wherein both partners can freely articulate their cultural heritage and convictions, devoid of concerns regarding external judgment, through the cultivation of tolerance.

It takes curiosity and effort to comprehend one another's cultural traditions and beliefs to exercise tolerance in a cross-cultural relationship. We should cherish the distinctiveness and variety that result from our diverse cultural backgrounds rather than seeing them as impediments. Couples that are tolerant of one another can respect one another's differences and collaborate to create something new that incorporates elements from their cultural heritages. Both individuals feel the experience has helped them develop and mature as people, strengthening the bond between partners.

Applying tolerance and empathy in multicultural collaborations significantly positively affects conflict resolution. When disagreements arise, partners who consistently practice empathy can better put themselves in their partner's shoes and see the issue from their partner's cultural viewpoint. They may now approach conflicts with empathy and a readiness to make concessions to get to a resolution that honors the cultural values of all parties. Additionally, tolerance facilitates this process by encouraging an open mindset and a willingness to compromise.

Additionally, compassion and tolerance transcend the couple's close, personal bond. Couples that embody these qualities are potent agents of societal change. They encourage others to be similarly tolerant and open-minded, which is advantageous for society. By emulating these traits in one another, couples may contribute to the world becoming a more tolerant and compassionate place.

It follows that the development of cross-cultural connections necessitates the practice of empathy and tolerance. They encourage an attitude of tolerance and mutual respect, which makes it simpler for couples to overcome challenges brought on by cultural differences. Couples may connect emotionally on a deeper level because empathy and tolerance teach them to respect and cherish the cultural identities of others. Couples that exhibit these qualities strengthen their bonds and inspire others to cherish and embrace diversity.

Moreover, the presence of compassion and understanding within multicultural relationships has implications that extend beyond the confines of the individuals involved. Couples exhibiting these particular attributes serve as catalysts within social contexts, fostering the development of a more inclusive and empathetic global society.

Couples exemplify a role model for others by demonstrating mutual acceptance and genuine care for each other. They motivate individuals to emulate their behavior by exemplifying tolerance, inclusivity, and acceptance through their conduct. The attainability of these goals is exemplified by couples who effectively embrace cultural differences and skillfully navigate the challenges they entail by applying empathy and understanding.

When these couples engage in social interactions with their networks of family, friends, and acquaintances, they generate a beneficial cascade effect. The dedication to exhibiting compassion and tolerance by individuals promotes the facilitation of constructive dialogue, the bridging of cultural disparities, and the unification of diverse individuals. Individuals often experience a shift in their pre-existing beliefs and perceptions surrounding diversity when they witness the genuine affection and mutual respect displayed among individuals from different cultural backgrounds.

The establishment of cross-cultural relationships necessitates the consistent demonstration of tolerance and comprehension. Couples who can empathize with each other demonstrate enhanced capacity in effectively addressing challenges from their culturally diverse backgrounds. In contrast, tolerance promotes an inclusive environment wherein individuals can freely manifest their cultural identities without apprehension of reproach or exclusion.

The capacity of a couple to understand and accept each other is crucial in developing a robust cross-cultural relationship. The individuals currently possess a deep understanding and respect for each other's cultural customs, perceiving their differences as valuable attributes rather than drawbacks. This not only fosters increased proximity among individuals but also promotes knowledge acquisition and information sharing.

The frequency and significance of cross-cultural encounters are rising in contemporary globalized society. The establishment and maintenance of these connections necessitate the consistent cultivation of empathy and tolerance. These relationships facilitate the development of a society characterized by enhanced peace and tolerance, wherein individuals from diverse backgrounds are esteemed.

Establishing and maintaining interpersonal connections among individuals from diverse backgrounds necessitates the cultivation of compassion and tolerance. Couples who demonstrate these attributes experience positive outcomes in their relationships and assume the role of catalysts for societal transformation within their communities. They promote the adoption of compassionate and inclusive perspectives, thereby enhancing the global condition. These two examples exemplify the profound impact of love in facilitating the dissolution of societal divisions and fostering solidarity among individuals from diverse backgrounds.

Establishing connections between different communities is a multifaceted endeavor that presents gratifying and demanding aspects. It necessitates the cultivation of qualities such as empathy and receptiveness. These identified characteristics can serve as a valuable framework for couples to navigate and derive advantages from cultural differences effectively.

Empathy is essential because it enables relationships and mutual learning. One must place themselves in the position of the other individual and experience what they are feeling and thinking. Partners who actively endeavor to understand and appreciate one another's perspectives foster an environment where everyone can feel heard, seen, and understood. A sense of closeness and connection can develop when one partner comprehends the cultural factors that influence the other's worldview.

It is impossible to overstate the importance of empathy in intercultural interactions. It helps individuals overcome their own biases and preconceptions about their partner's culture to recognize and respect their differences. If a couple can demonstrate empathy for one another, navigating cultural differences and misunderstandings will be simpler.

Tolerance, however, is essential for fostering an environment where everyone feels valued and at home. It is about relinquishing the need to alter or conform and embracing one another, flaws and all. Tolerant couples are more likely to appreciate and passionately embrace their cultural differences.

Couples who are tolerant of one another create an environment where individuals can be themselves without fear of being judged. Partners can discuss their backgrounds, traditions, and religious beliefs openly without fear of retaliation from their partners. Couples empathetic towards one another can better resolve culturally-based conflicts and reach compromises.

Compassion and tolerance foster friendship and intercultural understanding most effectively when combined. They foster an environment where companions can learn from one another and increase their respect, tolerance, and understanding of the world's diverse cultures. Couples can lay the groundwork for a lifetime of respect and understanding by practicing tolerance and compassion towards one another.

Cultivating empathy and tolerance is of greater benefit to cross-cultural relationships than to the individuals involved. Couples who demonstrate acceptance and tolerance encourage others to respect diversity and strive toward a more peaceful world. They transcend convention by demonstrating the universality of love and the strength of empathy and tolerance in forging enduring connections between individuals of all origins.

Developing empathy and tolerance is crucial for developing and maintaining cross-cultural interactions. Couples can strengthen their emotional connection and mutual understanding by cultivating empathy. Tolerance encourages couples to embrace their cultural differences and resolve conflicts amicably and with mutual respect. Collectively, these characteristics form the basis for positive relationships between individuals of disparate cultural backgrounds, promoting a more tolerant and compassionate global community.

When it comes to interactions between people from different cultures, using understanding and tolerance has benefits that go beyond the two people involved in the relationship. The act puts in motion a chain of good deeds that greatly impact the whole community, far beyond the immediate area of influence of the people involved.

Empathetic couples learn to understand and care about each other's problems and successes by looking at things from the same point of view as their partners. Because of their increased sensitivity, people can better support their partner's cultural background and help others accept it. Couples who talk about their lives and try to make others feel what they feel can help people in their communities be more accepting of differences.

The idea of tolerance is similar to the idea of acceptance in that it has the power to change the way people think and act in a group. When people in a relationship accept and appreciate each other's cultural differences, they can face unfair practices and preconceived ideas that keep bias alive. People's tendency to accept others helps build a compassionate society because it makes people think about their biases and encourages them to value differences. Couples who appreciate and accept each other's cultural differences can be used as examples of tolerance and understanding in their communities.

Also, couples who are good at navigating cross-cultural relationships do so by working for social change. By actively trying to learn about and appreciate each other's pasts, people encourage cultural exchange and the growth of their knowledge and experiences. Through meetings with people from other cultures and learning from each other, people can start new good traditions for everyone involved.

Couples from different cultural backgrounds who are good role models for tolerance and acceptance have a substantial influence beyond their immediate social networks. The romantic connection that developed between them is a fascinating illustration of how love can unite people who come from very different places and have different worldviews. They are illustrative of the concept that displays of liking and interpersonal relationships are not limited by geographical limits because of their unique personal encounters that defy societal norms. This is because their interactions have challenged societal conventions in ways that have challenged them personally. The bravery shown by people in the face of the challenges inherent in multicultural relationships acts as a source of inspiration for those close to them.

These couples actively contribute to the improvement of the overall well-being of society by the demonstration of compassion and love that they show toward their fellow community members. Interactions between people of different cultures are actively promoted and developed, playing a vital part in developing inclusive societies that respect and value the variety of cultural backgrounds in the world. Individuals contribute to developing a lasting sense of inclusion and cohesiveness among subsequent generations by acting in this manner.

Chapter 3: Love and Commitment

In this chapter, we will explore the significance of commitment in a partnership's long-term success and strength. We will emphasize commitment's crucial role in establishing a lasting and thriving bond. By exploring the intricate mechanics of commitment, we will examine how it enables relationships to withstand challenges, grow stronger, and deepen over time.

This chapter explores prevalent issues in marital relationships and delves into the role of love as a potential resolution. When a romantic partnership is driven by genuine affection, the couple's likelihood of overcoming obstacles and experiencing personal growth increases. The resilience exhibited by couples amid adversity serves as evidence of the profound impact of love, which has the potential to enable individuals to surmount seemingly insurmountable challenges.

The importance of fostering open communication and trust in establishing commitment is underscored. When a relationship is established upon a foundation of trust, it engenders a sense of safety and security for both individuals involved. Facilitating open communication and fostering mutual dependence, this practice simplifies the process of emotional expression and support between romantic partners during challenging circumstances. Effective communication facilitates problem-solving, fosters empathy, and enhances comprehension. It facilitates interpersonal communication among marital partners, resolving issues and articulating concerns. Couples have the potential to enhance their interpersonal bond through the practice of open communication and the cultivation of trust.

This chapter additionally emphasizes the significance of reciprocity within interpersonal relationships. A healthy relationship is characterized by the reciprocal exchange of affection and care between individuals. Harmony and reciprocity are fostered through individuals' demonstration of consideration towards each other's preferences and benevolence in their interactions. It cultivates authentic gratitude and recognition, reinforcing the commitment to the well-being and achievements of one another. Couples cultivate an atmosphere of reverence and gratitude by engaging in a reciprocal exchange of affection.

In this chapter, we offer guidance and strategies for enhancing the affection and dedication between partners amidst challenging circumstances. In this discourse, we explore strategies to enhance interpersonal connections, foster mutual understanding, and cultivate camaraderie. The fundamental elements of an enduring relationship encompass love, trust, open and sincere communication, and equitable sharing.

The amazing experiences of couples who have stayed together in the face of great hardships and adversity are a testament to the power of love and commitment. These couples demonstrate how love can endure and even bloom in adversity.

Love and commitment are conscious decisions that require time and dedication. By embracing the power of commitment, trust, open communication, and healthy trade, couples may create a relationship that not only endures but also thrives. The knowledge and tactics offered in this chapter enable readers to form a strong bond that will serve as the foundation of a successful lifetime partnership distinguished by love, compassion, and growth for both parties. Because love and commitment are not static notions, they necessitate constant development and adaptation. We recommend that married couples actively seek ways to improve their relationships by adopting a growth attitude. This can be accomplished through introspection, therapy, counseling, or relationship enrichment workshops. Couples may form a lasting bond by investing in each other's growth and the progression of their relationship.

In these inspiring stories, we meet couples who have won through loss and sadness, conflicts over ideas, and distinct but equal roads to success in their industries. These couples have shown their commitment to one another and their capacity to keep their love alive while enduring several obstacles together.

Individuals' hardships illustrate how love may increase their determination, bravery, and tenacity. Despite obstacles that may have caused them to divorce, these couples have shown their love for one another by remaining together.

Looking into the lives of people who have discovered love and loyalty in committed relationships illustrates the importance of these principles. These couples are more capable of communicating with one another than others. This improves their ability to empathize with one another and give comfort during stressful moments. It is widely accepted that love is ethereal and unachievable in the physical world. When we talk about resilience, we mean overcoming hardship, supporting one another, and working together to weather storms.

Individual experiences may teach people important lessons about tenacity and flexibility. Individuals in these partnerships have evolved, adapted to new situations, and learned that their shortcomings add to their strengths. They've grown closer due to their shared struggle, reinforcing their bond and preparing them for a happy future.

The tales of these amazing couples show how love and commitment can grow stronger in the face of tragedy. The difficulties they've faced as a group have strengthened their bond and heightened their devotion to one another. These couples' examples have the potential to tremendously inspire others, urging them to believe in love's capacity to better the world, to maintain relationships through difficulties, and to prioritize faithfulness above compromise.

Each couple's tale exemplifies the transformational power of love and commitment. These examples show how love transcends physical and temporal barriers. It is proved here that love lives outside of our thoughts. These couples' tenacity shows that love can help individuals overcome problems, make big adjustments, and attain permanent happiness. Loyalty's consequences on interpersonal interactions are also examined. To illustrate points, stories and real-world examples are utilized. In romantic comedies, the protagonists overcome their problems by supporting and caring for one another. These stories demonstrate the transformational power of love and unwavering dedication in the face of hardship.

Many difficulties might occur in the context of a romantic connection, including internal conflicts, poor decisions, external expectations, and shared responsibilities. On the other hand, love has a significant impact that may enable individuals in a committed relationship to grow closer to one another.

Couples frequently need help comprehending each other during communication. Unresolved conflicts, misunderstandings, and disputes in a relationship can hinder progress and make it more difficult to attain desired results. Real and open discussion is essential to overcome these obstacles, and love plays an important part in this.

Couples who approach discussions with love and a genuine desire to understand one another's points of view can bridge the gap, establish common ground, and settle disagreements.

When there is love in the relationship, both partners feel more comfortable opening out to one another. When two people are in love, they carefully listen to each other and consider their emotions, opinions, and points of view. As a result, you empathize with the other person and want to comprehend their point of view. When a partnership is built on love, they may communicate more effectively, making both parties feel heard and understood.

Problem-solving and conflict resolution are two other circumstances in which love is vital. When couples are motivated by love to resolve issues, they seek solutions that meet both of their needs while also addressing the requirements of the other. Love encourages active listening, in which both parties seek to comprehend what is stated and the underlying emotions and desires. Couples are thus more likely to communicate freely and openly about their experiences and perspectives on their relationships.

The existence of love also encourages sincerity and honesty in conversation. While love is the driving force in a relationship, each partner is more inclined to be open while talking. This risk taking contributes to the growth of trust and intimacy in partnerships. It allows partners to talk freely and work through challenges.

Couples can overcome the usual barriers to effective communication by employing love as a driving factor. When two people are truly in love, they may be entirely honest with one another without fear of rejection. It facilitates the process of mutual acquaintance and fosters personal development within a romantic relationship. When feelings of love drive couples, they exhibit enhanced abilities to surmount challenges, reconcile differences, and establish transparent and trustworthy communication channels.

The emotion of love catalyzes for partners to prioritize each other's needs through active listening and empathetic understanding. Rather than adopting a competitive mindset where one party emerges as the victor, deeply committed couples prioritize mutual understanding and collaborate to identify mutually beneficial solutions when faced with disagreements. This opposes couples who adopt an adversarial mindset where one partner seeks to emerge as the sole victor in disagreements. The individuals involved exhibit mutual respect's opinions, actively engage in attentive listening to each other's perspectives, and actively seek opportunities to identify shared interests or agreements. When two individuals experience a profound emotional connection, their inclination towards collaboration is heightened, leading them to actively seek resolutions to challenges and consider the needs and aspirations of their respective partners.

Love also fosters an environment in which individuals exhibit greater acceptance and reduced tendencies for criticism towards one another. Love has been found to have additional positive effects on society. Establishing a nurturing form of communication within the context of a marital relationship fosters an atmosphere wherein both individuals can express their authentic selves without the fear of causing harm or emotional distress to their partner.

In this setting, you'll find sincerity, openness, and the possibility of delving into deeper feelings and concepts. All of these qualities are there. When two people fall in love, they may learn to understand and admire one another's unique qualities and characteristics.

Having good social relationships helps you become a better listener. It encourages partners to concentrate not just on their verbal communication but also on the other person's needs, feelings, and concerns rather than just listening to what they say. Active listening tactics like paraphrasing, clarifying, and reflecting are frequently used by couples truly in love to enhance their link and ensure they both feel heard and understood.

When romantic love drives a couple, they are more likely to overcome the difficulties that prevent them from creating strong connections with others. Only the power of love can create a genuine and compassionate relationship between individuals. Couples may repair bridges, become emotionally closer, and learn to respect one another here. When two individuals speak with one another out of genuine concern for one another, they form the honest and deep emotional bond that distinguishes a good relationship. Partners may use this place to heal injured feelings, become emotionally closer, and inspire respect and appreciation in one another. A good relationship is built on an honest and deep emotional connection between partners, which may be nurtured via open and compassionate communication.

There are several factors outside of a relationship that can have a significant impact on it, such as work stress, money troubles, or family upheaval. Under such conditions, love can stimulate the developing of fortitude and endurance. Couples that work together share household responsibilities equitably and emotionally support one another are better prepared to deal with life's unforeseen twists and turns. A good love connection is marked by a commitment to one another and a readiness to support one another through difficult times.

The enduring impact of prior disasters or unresolved emotional traumas is a common issue for couples. It's worth emphasizing that love can hasten rehabilitation and promote improvement.

. Intimate connections are cultivated when couples participate in interactions characterized by benevolence and open-mindedness. Love is a powerful catalyst for facilitating personal transformation, as it empowers individuals to overcome obstacles and experience substantial growth in their emotional well-being. The existence of love within a romantic relationship can substantially impact the individual development and collective advancement of the parties involved.

Partnerships can need help stemming from disparate expectations, values, and interests. Couples are motivated by the emotional experience of love to appreciate and derive advantages from each other's unique perspectives. The acquisition of tolerance, comprehension, and conflict-resolution skills is important. Authentic love facilitates the transcendence of differences between two individuals, allowing them to embrace each other without any conditions wholeheartedly.

When two individuals are dedicated to one another, their mutual affection is a catalyst, providing both partners the strength to tackle hardship head-on. Couples that are open, sensitive, and capable of better understanding one another are better equipped to address difficulties jointly. When couples make love their guiding principle, they are more likely to overcome obstacles and grow closer to one another. Love is the core of a relationship because it exhibits tenacity in the face of adversity and perseverance throughout time.

The importance of honesty and transparency in developing loyalty is underlined. Establishing trust in a relationship is a critical step toward reaching those objectives. Transparency, honesty, and a strong belief in one's partner's genuine love and compassion are vital elements in a successful relationship. On the other hand, encouraging open and honest exchanges of views leads to increased learning, sympathy, and collaboration. It makes it simpler for couples to communicate their aspirations and dreams, which helps them feel more emotionally linked and ensures they both feel loved and respected.

We value developing a collaborative partnership based on an exchange that benefits both sides. To love someone, you must show them compassion, sympathy, and understanding daily.

It requires respecting one another's uniqueness and safety while looking after one another's emotional and physical well-being. Couples may develop a relationship built on mutual respect, gratitude, and support by balancing selfless actions and self-care.

We provide practical suggestions and exercises to help couples strengthen their commitment and establish the groundwork for a long-term relationship. We examine building trust by acting honestly, being dependable, and keeping your word. We also discuss effective communication skills for building stronger relationships and resolving conflicts amicably, such as active listening, empathy, and non-judgmental understanding.

One of the many important topics we cover is developing long-term strategies everyone agrees on. When partners coordinate their objectives, they develop a common identity and a sense of direction. Their joint goal motivates them to collaborate, strive, and progress personally and romantically. We educate couples on how to have honest and open conversations about their shared values, objectives, and future dreams to develop a strong foundation for their partnership.

Also discussed is the significance of prioritizing and making your relationship a priority. A passionate, loyal relationship requires time and work to maintain. Date nights, long chats, and other relationship-building activities are highly recommended. These planned interactions can help you develop emotional intimacy, memory sharing, and mutual understanding. The chapter delves into the idea that dedication is a journey rather than a destination. We talk about how important it is for married couples to reassess their commitment to one another regularly, especially in difficult situations. Couples who know that commitment involves effort are more equipped to work through difficulties and form stronger bonds.

The chapter underlines the need for perseverance in retaining commitment. The ability of a couple to overcome hurdles and remain loyal to one another in the face of adversity demonstrates the strength of their love. We discuss how building coping skills, seeking help when needed, and adopting a growth mindset that values change and development can help couples become more resilient.

There is debate over the need for giving and taking in keeping a commitment. It recognizes that no partnership is perfect and that things can always improve. Couples can discover common ground and work together to create solutions that benefit both parties by establishing an atmosphere of flexibility and compromise. To accomplish this, one must be willing to compromise, practice bargaining skills, and seek win-win alternatives.

Finally, in Chapter 3, couples are advised to regard their commitment to one another as a journey rather than a destination. It offers helpful hints and ways for cultivating the qualities required for any successful relationship: fortitude, open lines of communication, trust, and compromise. By following these rules, married couples can cultivate a love that endures over time and thrives despite the trials of life together.

Regarding self-care and personal growth, commitment is regularly brought up. Husbands and wives should prioritize their personal enjoyment and advancement over their marriage bond. We discuss the importance of supporting one another's aspirations, allowing one another to grow, and celebrating one another's accomplishments. This comprehensive approach enriches the connection as partners grow as individuals and as a pair.

We also discuss the necessity of being able to disagree politely as a group and having the tenacity to continue through adversities. How a couple handles conflict is a major predictor of their commitment to one another and overall satisfaction with their relationship. Active listening, expressing thoughts without criticizing others, seeking understanding, and generating win-win compromises are some of the conflict resolution strategies we teach. Couples can improve their bond and grow more confident in one another by resolving conflicts with empathy, respect, and a shared commitment to finding a solution.

We stress resolving conflicts while maintaining a joyful, playful, and spontaneous connection. Even though commitment necessitates genuine effort and accountability on both sides, it also necessitates a healthy amount of fun and excitement. The connection can be strengthened by pursuing similar hobbies, sharing new experiences, and discovering unexpected delights. Couples who surround themselves with happiness, joy, and shared laughter can develop long-lasting memories and a strong bond.

Importance of trust as the foundation of commitment. Openness, vulnerability, and emotional intimacy can exist only in a relationship built on a solid basis of trust. Being dependable, consistent, and keeping your commitments are crucial in a partnership. This promotes the growth of trust between couples, making it easier for them to commit to one another completely.

A good relationship also depends on the parties involved sharing the same values and viewpoints. When a couple has similar beliefs and viewpoints, they feel more connected to one another and are better able to communicate. To ensure they are on the same page, couples must talk honestly about their values, views, and goals. They are more likely to stick together if they have the same opinions. Gratitude and pleasure should always be expressed to one another. Two people may get closer and more devoted when they acknowledge and value one another's efforts, abilities, and talents. Your connection will get stronger if you consistently show your lover your thanks and worth. Being reliable, having compatible beliefs, and showing appreciation are thus essential elements of a durable, fulfilling partnership.

This chapter also emphasizes the importance of empathy and compassion in maintaining a relationship. To truly love someone, you must be willing to stand by them through good and terrible times. Discussions center on showing compassion, paying close attention while listening, and sustaining your relationship. A trusting and open environment can assist a couple's emotional ties, and commitment flourish.

The chapter also examines the role of jointly practiced rituals and customs in maintaining allegiance. What matters most are the rituals and conventions that marriage builds over time. Activities like this bring couples closer together because they foster a sense of community and the development of lasting memories. These traditions encourage recommitment, introspection, and companionship.

The significance of meditation and growth in fidelity is also discussed. Each individual's development promotes the partnership's energy and overall health. We encourage committed relationships that promote mutual development via self-awareness and personal growth. Couples that invest in their growth strengthen their bond with one another and grow closer as a result.

It underlines the dynamic nature of commitment and the value of emotional support, compromise, and personal development. This chapter teaches partners how to cultivate these characteristics to create a lasting connection. A couple can develop a strong and enduring commitment that lasts throughout their journey together by adopting the ideas and strategies presented in this chapter.

Reflection and growth play a role in keeping a relationship's foundation of trust and commitment. It underlines how each partner's development contributes to the overall success of the collaboration. We encourage committed relationships that promote mutual development via self-awareness and personal growth.

By reflecting on themselves, people can better understand themselves and their interests, needs, and motivations. This understanding allows individuals to communicate more honestly and openly with their partner, which improves their emotional bond. It also allows them to evaluate their personal growth potential and focus on changing negative actions or attitudes that may impede their relationship.

Furthermore, as a person matures, they bring new interests, activities, and views to the partnership. Each member's pursuit of personal interests, development of personal abilities, and pursuit of personal passions improves the partnership. As a result, people become more devoted to the relationship since they enjoy and are proud of their development, which benefits the partnership.

As a

result of self-improvement initiatives, partners are inspired and motivated to aid and foster the progress of one another. When a couple acknowledges each other's efforts and accomplishments while providing feedback and support, they create an environment that encourages growth and dedication.

Couples prioritizing introspection and growth create an environment where both partners can thrive. Investing in one another's development benefits both partners and the partnership. It strengthens couples' relationships through conquering hurdles, accepting change, and growing as a team.

When partners emphasize self-reflection and personal improvement, they create an atmosphere that fosters both spouses' pleasure and growth. Couples who help each other succeed show how much they care about their happiness and success. They can overcome obstacles and cope with life's constant flux because of their dedication.

Couples that spend time getting to know themselves better via reflection will be able to connect and communicate with one another more effectively. They may find growth opportunities and apply that knowledge to become their best selves. Each partner's continual growth and development improves the partnership by adding new perspectives, insights, and talents.

Couples that prioritize reflection value their own and their partner's personal development. They create a pleasant environment where both partners are driven to pursue their dreams and goals. A partner can help their spouse in various ways, including emotional support, feedback, and active participation in their progress. Couples can strengthen their bonds and find common ground by supporting and celebrating one another's victories.

Emphasizing introspection and personal growth as a pair also helps the relationship progress. Couples committed to progress are more likely to acknowledge their concerns, work to resolve them, and eventually get closer. They argue that maintaining a contented and joyful marriage takes consistent work, research, and modification.

Relationships prioritizing self-awareness and personal growth substitute an environment of collaboration, fulfillment, and ongoing improvement. They develop their connections, mutual respect, and feeling of purpose by assisting one another in growing. Couples committed to development can overcome obstacles, adjust to new circumstances, and form lasting ties. A couple can establish a strong, meaningful, long-lasting relationship through mutual self-reflection and progress.

Any relationship's health, longevity, and overall success are directly proportional to the degree to which both parties are willing to give and receive. A feeling of reciprocity and contentment can be fostered in a relationship through the equal exchange of care, support, and understanding between partners. It takes a mindset that is open, flexible, and willing to compromise to acknowledge that each partner has their own individual requirements, wishes, and ideas and the willingness to meet each other halfway.

A partnership can achieve equity and justice when both parties maintain an attitude of kindness and altruism. It acknowledges the significance and worth of the requirements and requirements of each partner. When spouses take turns listening and empathizing with one another, they foster an atmosphere in which everyone feels that they are being heard, valued, and respected. This deepens the emotional connection between you and the other person and encourages collaboration and partnership rather than competition.

Being willing to accept and provide gifts is beneficial to both the individual and the company. Within the confines of the partnership, it makes room for each person's identity and particular ambitions and interests. Any committed partnership needs to provide room for growth while allowing each partner to keep their identity intact. It is optional for couples to choose between their satisfaction as individuals or as a cohesive unit and their pleasure within the context of their relationship.

When people are willing to give and take, the conditions are set for developing a culture that values compromise, problem-solving, and constructive conflict resolution. Conflicts and differences are inevitable in any relationship; nevertheless, the ability of the partners to discover areas of agreement and work together to produce solutions beneficial to both sides allows the partnership to endure and thrive. Couples willing to give and take have a better chance of successfully negotiating, bargaining, and cooperating to find solutions that benefit both parties. This activity fosters group cohesion, collaborative decision-making, and improved awareness of each other's requirements and preferences.

Giving and receiving on an equal level implies that both parties are invested in the expansion and prosperity of the partnership. If you want to make the happiness and satisfaction of your partners your first priority, you will need to demonstrate initiative, empathy, and compassion. When partners actively seek strategies to support, uplift, and celebrate one another, loving relationships have a better chance of flourishing. This fosters closeness, trust, and a powerful emotional connection between you.

To conclude, to keep a relationship healthy over time, both parties must be willing to sacrifice for the other. When a person's partner lives up to their expectations and acknowledges their goals, the relationship has a greater feeling of fairness, equality, and equilibrium. When a couple can successfully communicate with one another, work through issues together, and locate areas of common ground, they are better prepared to deal with challenges and arguments in their relationship. By taking on this perspective, couples can engage in more conversation and work together, laying the framework for a healthy and stable relationship.

Chapter 4: How to Increase Your Love Through Talking

This chapter examines the role of effective conversation in fostering interpersonal connections and enhancing individuals' experience of affection. To improve interpersonal relationships and promote mutual understanding, engaging in candid and transparent communication regarding our thoughts and emotions is imperative.

Successful and healthy relationships are established upon the foundation of open communication. Effective communication in romantic relationships fosters understanding and promotes emotional well-being. Engaging in open and honest dialogue with our partners allows them to gain insight into our desires, values, and concerns. Effective communication enhances interpersonal relationships by facilitating improved responsiveness from our partners, fostering more substantial and meaningful connections.

Inadequate and deficient communication frequently results in misinterpretations and conflicts. In situations where individuals are unable to articulate their intended message effectively, it can result in a range of negative consequences, including but not limited to confusion, irritation, and potential harm to interpersonal connections. Efforts to enhance dialogue can effectively mitigate the likelihood of miscommunication and conflicts among individuals.

Interpersonal conflicts can be reduced by enhancing our ability to articulate our thoughts and intentions effectively. Active listening, comprehension, and effective communication are three paramount skills that can be acquired. Active listening involves directing our attention towards the speaker and consciously comprehending their perspective without interrupting or presuming. Individuals are likely to experience increased comfort in expressing their thoughts and emotions, enhancing their propensity to communicate their sentiments openly.

Individuals can gain insight into and establish connections with their partner's cognitive and affective experiences by cultivating empathy. Acknowledging that their objectives and desires may not invariably align with our own is imperative. Heart plays a crucial role in facilitating effective communication, enabling individuals to comprehend and demonstrate concern for one another.

The ability to express one's emotions is equally vital. It's critical that we can explain our wishes, demands, and limitations clearly and nicely. To do so, we must adopt assertive communication tactics, such as stating our opinions without regard for what others may think. By being explicit in our communication, we empower our partners to respond to us with empathy and compassion.

A desire to deal with challenges and arguments constructively is also required for better communication in our relationships. In any close connection, conflict is unavoidable, but how we handle it significantly impacts the bond we form. Active listening, compromise, and finding win-win solutions are all ways to resolve problems in a way that does not jeopardize the relationship between the persons involved.

Every successful conversation necessitates active listening. Respect, empathy, and a willingness to comprehend the other person's point of view are all conveyed via attentive listening. By developing trust and promoting honest dialogue, active listening provides a comfortable environment where both parties may feel at ease opening up to one another.

Open and honest communication allows for the resolution of differences and the establishment of compromises. When we are straightforward about what we want and need, we offer ourselves and our relationships the space to work through challenges and discover mutually beneficial solutions. We can overcome our differences and become closer through an open and honest debate.

Excellent verbal and nonverbal communication skills are required for effective communication. These include paying attention to our body language, making direct eye contact, and utilizing clear, straightforward language. Another attribute that may aid in creating a supportive and caring environment in a relationship is the capacity to empathize and understand people.

Finally, open and honest communication is essential for developing and sustaining successful interpersonal connections. We may strengthen our relationships with our partners, work through our differences, and establish a happier and loving relationship if we value open and honest expression, attentive listening, and the development of good communication skills.

Having candid dialogues allows partners to become more emotionally linked. We create a place for emotional connection by expressing our ideas, feelings, and vulnerabilities with our partners. Being transparent with our relationships allows them to understand us better and give us the comfort we require.

Open communication channels aid in forming and maintaining trust in cooperation. Honesty and transparency in communication, which demonstrate integrity and reliability, are the foundation for building trust. Trust is developed, and the relationship grows when both parties can talk honestly without fear of being misunderstood or retaliated against.

Effective problem-solving also requires clear communication. We can discuss difficulties or arguments and come up with solutions if we communicate openly and honestly. If we listen to each other, we can work together to discover solutions that benefit everyone. This strategy strengthens partner ties by fostering problem-solving teamwork.

Open communication promotes a welcoming and caring workplace. When we are upfront and honest with our partners about what we need, want, and can and cannot tolerate, they are more positioned to help us. Similarly, when we pay attention and display empathy, our partners feel more comfortable opening up and disclosing their feelings. Their mutual support enhances their closeness and fondness for one another.

An open communication atmosphere at work promotes strong relationships among coworkers. Coworkers can help us more effectively if we are open and honest about our needs, expectations, and boundaries. When people are at ease enough to honestly communicate their views and emotions, a culture of open discourse and respect can emerge.

Actively exercising empathy at work can have a significant impact on coworker relationships. When we try to hear what others say, show interest in what they say, and express empathy, we create an environment in which others feel secure opening up. When team members feel understood and cared for, they are more inclined to work efficiently and enjoy one another's presence.

Intimacy and attachment flourish when coworkers can confide in one another and provide sympathetic support. When employees are involved in decision-making and believe their ideas matter, they are more likely to become invested in the organization. A caring and supportive workplace can boost employee morale, job satisfaction, and well-being, increasing productivity and teamwork.

Open communication is also necessary for addressing challenges at work. Disputes can be handled more quickly if people communicate their differences openly and honestly. To improve understanding and problem resolution through conversation and compromise, we must establish an environment where people feel safe expressing their opinions and concerns without fear of punishment.

Establishing and maintaining love relationships depend on open and honest communication. It promotes trust, closeness, and understanding in relationships and allows people to communicate with one another on a deeper level. Practical cooperation is built on open and honest communication between parties.

Honest conversation is the key to building solid relationships, so it's essential to encourage reliable information sharing. Here are a few good ways to make it easier for people to trust each other.

The first step is to make sure everyone feels safe and at ease. To get better at this skill, you need to understand how the other person feels, not talk over them, and not reject or criticize their point of view. When people feel safe and essential, they are more likely to talk about their thoughts and feelings.

Second, being able to listen carefully is a vital part of building trust. Active listening shows you care about what the other person has to say. This means keeping eye contact, showing through words and body language that you understand, and, if necessary, asking for more information. By showing interest in what the other person has to say, we could earn their trust and let them talk quickly, and ethics are the building blocks of faith. When we are open and honest with each other, people can believe what we say and mean. When we talk freely and honestly, we show that we are sincere and have integrity, two traits necessary for building trust in relationships. It would help if you never lay or misrepresent something because it hurts confidence and shuts down free speech.

To build trust, you need to do things reliably and consistently. Trust is built slowly over time through constant follow-through, keeping promises, and reliable behavior. Reliability and trustworthiness create an atmosphere where people feel safe sharing personal information and discussing sensitive topics.

One way to build trust is to be careful with personal information and data. We respect the other person's privacy by keeping secret any information they tell us in confidence. When people can talk to each other freely and frankly without worrying about being misunderstood or led astray, they can form stronger ties.

Information talks that build trust are also helped by constructive feedback and not being on the defensive. Instead of criticizing the person, positive and encouraging feedback helps to build trust by focusing on specific behaviors or situations. Also, show that you can be trusted and encourage ongoing conversation by reacting to feedback without getting defensive and being open to learning and growing.

For trustworthy information exchanges to happen, people need to be able to give and take helpful feedback, listen carefully, be sincere and honest, be consistent and reliable, respect privacy and confidentiality, and not judge. By using these methods, we can build trust and have more open conversations, strengthening our relationships.

Also, patience and understanding are needed to build trust in how people share knowledge. Faith can't be made or made to happen by force. It has to be earned and grown over time. One's ability to trust is affected by their flaws and what they've been through. Being patient and understanding lets trust grow naturally, giving each person the time and space they need to feel safe sharing information.

It takes time and work to earn and keep someone's trust. Each person's ability to trust is affected by their strengths, flaws, and traumatic events. I've learned that building confidence is a tricky process that takes time, care, and understanding.

If I approach it quietly and kindly, I can allow folks to share knowledge at their speed. Some people take longer than others to feel safe enough to talk, especially if their trust has been broken. By being gentle, I create a safe place where people can be honest and share their knowledge openly.

Also, understanding is essential for building trust. I put myself in other people's shoes because I know everyone has experiences and problems that may make it hard for them to trust and talk freely with others. When I have empathy, I can understand and validate their feelings, which makes them feel cared for and loved. This understanding makes it possible for both safety and trust to grow.

Building trust is not a one-time goal but something you do every day. To reach this goal, one must always act in the same way, talk honestly, and be ready to solve any problems or mistakes that may come up. I can help you because I've been friendly and patient during this challenging time of building trust.

Trust in the sharing of information takes time and patience. Maintaining someone's trust takes time and work, and you can't force or rush the process. By being patient, I give people the space and time to open up and talk, making them feel more comfortable and improving their trust in me. People may also be more likely to trust each other if they are kind to each other and aware of how their own lives affect those around them. I can build trusted relationships that let me share knowledge freely and openly by being patient and understanding.

For people to trust you, you have to show that you care. When we know what the other person is going through, how they feel, and what they want, we can relate to them and build a bond with them. Empathy for someone else shows that you care about their feelings and builds trust, which is both important for real and honest conversation.

We may also build trust when we own up to our mistakes and take responsibility for our actions. We must own up to our errors and truly apologize when we unintentionally harm someone with our words or behavior. We should also try to make things better. To build and keep trust in a relationship, both sides must take responsibility for their actions and be open to feedback and ways to grow.

To build trust, you need to talk about limits regularly and openly. When we talk about and value each other's personal space, we create an environment where everyone can feel safe and at ease. People are more likely to trust each other when they know their boundaries and opinions. Respecting limits shows that we want to create a safe, respectful space where people can talk openly.

Lastly, you must show you can be trusted to build a good image. Being on time, keeping our word, and being dependable are all significant parts of building relationships. Being reliable shows people they can trust us and gives them confidence that what they think about our motives is right.

Building dependable relationships through information sharing requires patience, understanding, responsibility, openness about limits, and unshakable dependability. Doing these things can create a trusting environment where communication soars, leading to stronger ties and better relationships.

I've often seen how debate can overcome divides and strengthen ties between people. These instances demonstrate the need to speak up to bridge gaps and build understanding.

Two people best demonstrate this I know now who are having problems in their love relationships. These people prefer an open conversation in which they may openly express their opinions and feelings. They created trust and allowed one another to open up to them by listening to one another and conversing honestly and freely. They learned new things about one another, found places of agreement, and renewed their ability for empathy and compassion via these conversations. They were able to reconcile their disagreements and increase their understanding of one another via open dialogue, paving the way for a more profound and genuine friendship.

Another heartwarming story includes a group of friends who separated for various reasons. Instead of allowing their relationships to deteriorate, they got together and had an honest chat. Everyone was allowed to express themselves and was given uncritical hearing and understanding. They overcome these challenges by working together to clear the air, apologize, and move on. They learned to appreciate each member's unique contributions, which strengthened their bonds and helped them rebuild their ties.

I've seen how open communication within families has benefitted relationships and how they deal with difficult situations. Finally, family members who had been avoiding one another or harboring grudges determined to talk honestly with one another. They could reestablish trust and create a more sympathetic and supportive environment by listening to one another's perspectives, sharing their concerns, and talking about what they wished. Conflicts were handled, mutual understanding was developed, and the family was brought closer together by stressing open communication.

These real-world examples demonstrate how communication may assist in breaking down barriers and fostering trust. Through free dialogue, people may argue their differences, acquire understanding from one another's experiences, and finally uncover grounds for agreement. An honest debate of conflicting ideas may help mend fences, increase empathy, and deepen bonds, all of which contribute to mutual understanding and long-term peace.

People who communicate openly are better equipped to understand one another, collaborate to solve problems, and progress as individuals and as a group. When individuals talk openly and honestly with one another, they can better understand their own prejudices and beliefs. They can learn to question their assumptions and biases, learn more, and build better empathy and understanding.

Discussions also promote collective decision-making and collaboration. When individuals get together to address their disagreements, they can strive to find solutions and compromises that meet everyone's interests and desires. This method develops connections and promotes cooperation and accountability for results.

Importantly, open communication fosters an environment where everyone feels comfortable expressing their views. People are more willing to speak openly and honestly when they believe their opinions have been heard, recognized, and understood. This encourages the development of deeper ties and genuine intimacy by creating an environment in which being open and vulnerable is appreciated.

Honest communication has far-reaching consequences that go beyond the persons concerned. It provides an example of how to interact with one another and handle disputes constructively, which other couples may find valuable. We can influence society to progress toward more constructive and helpful contact if we all speak up, share our stories, and encourage others to do the same.

Real-life instances of how open discourse has helped individuals resolve their differences and grow closer to one another highlight the transforming power of honest and truthful communication. Because it encourages cooperation, personal growth and develops an environment of trust and respect, open communication may aid in establishing more strong relationships between individuals and a more harmonious society. By interacting, we may learn to understand one another and form long-lasting ties that benefit not just ourselves but others around us.

By practicing active listening and empathetic conduct, I may improve the quality of my interactions with others and the strength of my connections. While actively listening, I participate in the conversation and give the other person my attention. This entails actively paying attention, keeping eye contact, and responding appropriately in response to verbal and nonverbal signals. By paying attention, I create a pleasant environment where people can freely express themselves by displaying my admiration for their points of view and reinforcing their sentiments.

Empathy is required for good communication. To develop empathy, I put myself in the shoes of others and acquire their thoughts, beliefs, and desires. Paying attentive attention to the spoken words and the speaker's voice tone, facial expressions, and other nonverbal indicators is required. I may indicate that I care about the other person and their feelings by reacting with attention and kindness.

Stronger bonds may be formed, and mutual understanding can be developed if I actively listen and sympathize with others. As a result of my attentive listening, I can better understand what is being said and avoid misconceptions. As a result, the speaker is more comfortable speaking freely and expressing their opinions. Because of my compassionate responses, people trust me and feel more at ease during in-depth talks.

As a consequence of my usage of active listening and empathy, my ability to handle disputes and confrontations has increased. If I truly understand the other person's point of view and feelings, I may reply with empathy and discover a common ground for resolution. It helps me approach arguments cooperatively and seek solutions that benefit all parties rather than focusing on winning or proving my point. This promotes beneficial dialogue and helps maintain the vital link during difficult times.

Finally, I can better relate to others and express myself through active listening and empathy. I foster trust and open communication by giving the speaker my undivided attention. I can connect to others more intimately when I know their ideas, feelings, and experiences and respond appropriately. Because of these skills, I can now manage conflicts more successfully, have more confidence in other people, and establish better, more rewarding connections with others.

Furthermore, by engaging in active listening and empathy activities, I can better understand people's underlying needs and feelings. People may struggle to express their sentiments or hide their concerns for fear of being judged. I can understand people's underlying emotions and intentions by paying close attention to what they say and putting myself in their shoes. This allows me to address the main issue and support the other person in ways that would be difficult in a brief talk.

Furthermore, attentively listening and demonstrating empathy makes the other person feel acknowledged and cherished. When I pay attention to what they're saying and confirm that I understand them, I may show that I value the other person's perspectives and experiences. When people receive this kind of support, they are motivated to reveal more of their actual selves because they feel safe enough to be themselves. In this context, people may be themselves without caring about what other people think.

Active listening and empathy aid in the development of rapport. People are more inclined to do the same for me if I genuinely try to hear and comprehend their point of view. Listening and empathizing alternatively strengthen the communication dynamic, producing an environment of respect and collaboration.

Finally, I've learned that improving my communication skills by combining active listening and empathy has helped me feel more connected to people, attend to their needs, and advance myself. If I am present, empathetic, and sensitive, I can facilitate good communication beyond words, resulting in greater understanding, mutual respect, and stronger bonds.

It's hard to overstate how critical unconscious cues like body language are in building connections with other people. The more people I talk to, the more I realize that words only sometimes do an excellent job of capturing all the different ways people feel. Body language, facial emotions, and other nonverbal cues can tell much about a person's goals and feelings in a given scenario. When I pay attention to these signs, I can figure out how someone feels from what they say. When I know these signs, I can react to other people's needs and act with care. Nonverbal cues can also help people get to know and trust each other. You can show interest and attention by making eye contact, nodding in agreement, and matching the other person's body language. People get along better because these behavioral cues help build trust and comfort. By watching and reacting to people's unconscious cues and body language, I can learn more about them and grow closer to them.

Also, body language and unconscious cues make communication possible even if you don't speak the same language or come from the same country. Nonverbal cues, on the other hand, are usually global and may be understood by people from various cultures without the need for translation. If you can't say what you want to say, a warm smile, a gentle touch, or a nod of agreement might be enough. This way of communicating without words may help people from different backgrounds get along better because they don't have to use words.

Also, talks are more exciting and challenging when people use nonverbal cues like body language. In addition to words, they can send complex ideas and higher levels of knowledge. During an intense conversation, for example, a gentle touch on the arm can show concern and support, strengthening the bond between the two people. During a talk, it's essential to keep making eye contact with the other person to build a comfortable level of trust and connection.

Also, facial cues are often a reliable way to tell if someone is being honest. Most nonverbal cues are natural and unplanned, while words can be picked or handled intentionally. People's body language and facial reactions frequently show genuine emotions—happiness, sadness, or worry. These signs help me determine if a person is being honest about how they feel and what they want, leading to more open and honest talks.

Lastly, people can learn more about each other by reading their body language and other unconscious cues. They add depth to dialogue, show understanding, break down societal barriers, and let you know how someone feels. I can better understand and connect with people when I pay attention to and use facial cues in my talks.

In a relationship, body language and other unconscious cues are often used to make someone feel at ease. When people know how to read each other's body language, they may talk more freely and understand each other's thoughts. When someone is upset or weak, a kind word or a comforting hug can help them feel better and regain their confidence. Knowing these unconscious cues lets me support and praise someone without having to talk for a long time. In a close-knit group, each bond gets more substantial and mentally connected.

More strong bonds and mutual ease can be fostered by carefully studying and applying nonverbal cues such as body language. People are more inclined to communicate honestly and openly when comprehending one another's nonverbal cues.

A person's nonverbal cues can reveal much about their mental state and mood. This realization allows us to modify our actions in a way that consistently leaves the other person feeling heard and valued. When we detect fear in another person, we can offer reassurance or create a secure environment in which they can vent their concerns.

In times of emotional difficulty or vulnerability, the power of a kind word or a comforting embrace cannot be emphasized. These small gestures of support can have a significant impact and help the recipient feel more at ease. If we learn to read and react to these nonverbal cues, we can provide support and encouragement without needing a drawn-out conversation. Using nonverbal clues to encourage and affirm someone when words fail if they can't express their feelings is helpful.

Members of a close-knit group develop relationships and a more profound psychological connection by picking up on and reacting to one another's nonverbal clues. When everyone in a group is on the same page and understanding each other, the dynamic becomes more supportive and trustworthy. Strengthening group cohesion and members' sense of belonging can be achieved by emphasizing and interpreting nonverbal indicators.

You can also use nonverbal cues to determine how interested and engaged someone is. Leaning in, keeping your body language open, and nodding your head are great ways to show interest and attention to what's being said. Using these nonverbal cues, the other person may see I'm involved and paying attention to our talk. When both people use silent signs, the relationship strengthens, making more in-depth conversations possible.

Also, silent cues are especially good at communicating feelings when words aren't available. When there are language problems, like in cross-cultural relationships or when talking to someone who doesn't speak much English, nonverbal cues are even more critical. People who don't speak the same language can still bond and feel understanding through smiles, handshakes, and sympathy.

Lastly, body language and other forms of nonverbal speech are essential for building bonds with others. They give us peace, help us understand ourselves and others, show that someone is paying attention to us, and go beyond the limits of words. My ability to connect with more people and use social cues well opens the door to stronger relationships and ties that last longer. Research shows that silent cues are a big part of how we communicate daily and may be more important than what we say. It has been demonstrated that showing feelings and attitudes through actions rather than words is more effective than just using words.

Body language, tone of voice, and facial gestures add depth and meaning to communication. They can add nuance to a sentence, draw attention to important parts, or help the reader understand. A simple nod of agreement strengthens the connection and clarifies that both people understand what is being said.

Just as important as what someone says is what they do or don't say. When what we say and what we do match up, we look more honest and reliable. Consistent makes it more likely that the other person will believe what we say and do. If two people's physical cues don't match, it can lead to miscommunication or distrust, which makes it hard for them to talk to each other.

Nonverbal signs can be used to measure and understand how a conversation is going. They can tell people when to talk or stop, show interest or lack of interest, and help people take turns talking. I might change how I speak to you if I pay attention to these signs so that we can keep a respectful tone of voice.

It's important to remember that people and countries use different physical signs. To understand and react to nonverbal cues correctly, you must be aware of regional differences and your tastes. My ability to notice details and listen carefully will help me deal with these differences and build bridges between cultures.

Body language and other unconscious cues significantly affect how intense, deep, and wide a talk is. They help people understand better, build relationships, and connect with others. If I pay close attention to their nonverbal cues and react correctly, I may improve my social skills, kindness, and ability to make long-term connections with other people.

Chapter 5: Love and Sacrifice

This chapter explains why and how putting the other person's needs before your own can strengthen your romantic bond. Through exchanging personal experiences and reflections, we consider how selflessness may enrich relationships and transform individuals.

Being selfless in a romantic context involves more than just making adjustments or offering assistance to the other person. To truly love someone is to prioritize their needs and desires above your own. Focusing on the other person, considering their perspective, and responding empathetically is essential. When we prioritize our partners' needs over our own, we help them to feel loved and secure.

We also discuss how prioritizing others might improve your social life. Always being present for your partner fosters a sense of trust and security. In this attempt, we should prioritize humility and a genuine desire to make our spouse happy over ego, pride, and self-centered desires.

Treating others kindly benefits society as a whole. Supporting a partner is being excited for them and believing in their potential. Contributing to their development without expecting anything in return improves and strengthens our relationship.

In this chapter, you'll get advice on how to be less selfish in your romantic relationships. We discuss the significance of attentiveness, consideration, and self-care. We discuss the challenges of humility and its potential benefits. We also discuss the benefits of prioritizing our partner's demands over our own.

When we prioritize our partners' needs over our own, we strengthen our connection with them and lay the groundwork for a lifelong bond characterized by mutual love, trust, and support. Learning the meaning of true love and the beauty of nurturing a vibrant relationship with another person is best accomplished through selflessness.

In this chapter, we explore what it means to be unselfish in a romantic relationship and the benefits and drawbacks of prioritizing your partner's needs over your own. Most individuals believe that genuine generosity necessitates balancing self-care and social responsibility.

A couple's bond can be strengthened when partners give without expecting anything. Relationships are founded on trust, gratitude, and mutual aid when prioritizing the other person's well-being and success. When people go out of their way to help one another without asking for anything in return, they create an environment where it's simple to kick back and have a good time.

Kindness frequently has unintended outcomes. Remember to consider your requirements to assist others. Prioritizing your partner's requirements is essential, as is the ability to communicate your desires, emotions, and boundaries. Open and trustworthy communication is required to achieve a healthy balance between aiding others and caring for oneself.

Compassion in interpersonal interactions facilitates problem-solving and conflict resolution. Selfless individuals are better able to manage diversity and adversity. This results in mutually beneficial learning, concentration, and solutions for all parties. You and your companion could surmount obstacles and grow closer.

This chapter describes measures to become less selfish in romantic relationships. We stress the importance of frank communication, listening to one another, and mutual support. When one spouse prioritizes the other's needs, love, sagacity, and comprehension flourish between them.

Consider the importance of altruism in your alliances and relationships as you conclude this chapter. Putting your partner's requirements before your own may result in long-term happiness and satisfaction.

This chapter explores the lives of those who made significant sacrifices for the benefit of their loved ones. These fantastic activities demonstrate how far people will go to show their concern. They illustrate how important it is in committed relationships to put the needs of one's partner ahead of one's own.

We have seen and heard about individuals who have sacrificed for love in fiction and reality. To be with their partner, they may relocate far away, prioritize their partner's needs over their own, or switch careers to better provide for their family. These selfless acts disclose people's profound affection for their romantic relationships.

The chapter also examines the impact of these sacrifices on the partnership. Engaging in acts of sacrifice for one's romantic partner can fortify the emotional connection between individuals, enhance their commitment and reliance on one another, and propel their relationship to unprecedented growth and development. These acts of altruism establish the foundation for a collaborative alliance founded upon reciprocal comprehension, cooperation, and shared principles.

It is important to emphasize that within a partnership, no individual should experience a sense of obligation to make a concession. Effective and transparent communication regarding objectives, anticipations, and limitations is imperative for both partners to make concessions and understand each other's perspectives comprehensively and willingly. Healthy and harmonious relationships are established through mutual support and consideration for each partner's needs.

The present chapter elucidates remarkable instances of sacrificial acts driven by love, intending to inspire the reader. The cases above illustrate the profound influence that selflessness can exert on individuals and its transformative effect on interpersonal dynamics. This prompts contemplation regarding how much individuals are willing to sacrifice for their loved ones and the subsequent impact on their interpersonal connections.

Also, an examination is conducted on the potential challenges and complexities that may arise in love relationships due to individuals exhibiting selflessness. Making sacrifices for the sake of love can significantly alter an individual's life trajectory. However, it also presents a plethora of challenges and obstacles. Individuals are required to address these challenges through effective communication, exhibiting mutual respect, and prioritizing their welfare.

This chapter delves into the concept of selflessness in harmony, emphasizing the importance of prioritizing one's identity, growth, and happiness over those of one's partner. To minimize resentment, imbalance, and identity loss due to sacrifices, reasonable boundary establishment, self-care, and communication are stressed.

The chapter also acknowledges that selflessness in relationships extends well beyond heroic acts or enormous sacrifices. It involves little behaviors, such as expressing gratitude, extending a helping hand, and being considerate, that add up to establishing a happy and healthy relationship. Daily compromise, attentive listening, and sacrifice can strengthen any connection from the ground up.

The most crucial factor to remember while considering selflessness in romantic relationships is the depth and power of love. It underlines the importance of putting one's spouse first and one's actions impact on their life. Couples can create a strong bond built on trust, compassion, and mutual progress by putting their spouse's needs ahead of their own.

This chapter prompts the reader to reflect upon their level of compassion and its significance within their interpersonal connections. It is often emphasized that individuals should demonstrate affection and make selfless gestures towards their spouses without harboring any expectations of reciprocity. This will facilitate establishing a relationship founded upon mutual respect, support, and loyalty principles.

This section elucidates the poignant narratives of individuals who sacrificed for those they held dear.

Individuals prioritizing advancing their significant others' objectives over their aspirations are frequently commended. The acts mentioned above of benevolence demonstrate a remarkable dedication and exemplify the extent to which affection can compel individuals to sacrifice significantly for those they hold dear.

When individuals are informed about individuals who have voluntarily dedicated their time and exerted their energy to assist their families during illness or other challenging circumstances, they are consistently emotionally affected and express gratitude. These individuals have altruistically contributed financial resources, personal time, and various other forms of assistance without harboring any expectations of reciprocation. People who consistently help and support each other show what love is all about.

As you read these stories, you can't help but think about how much we can care for others and how far we would go to protect the people who are important to us. Because of this, people have to figure out how best to express their thoughts. These stories warn that love is a powerful force that can significantly change our lives and those we care about.

This chapter serves as a reminder of how much courage, strength, and commitment love can inspire. These stories of selflessness enhance our lives, strengthen our relationships with our loved ones, and touch our hearts by reminding us of the incredible power of love.

We are witnessing the great depth of loyalty and its terrible impact on relationships as we continue to delve into the heartbreaking stories of people who have given much to the ones they love. These people prioritize the well-being of their loved ones above all else and are incredibly philanthropic.

In many situations, one or both partners give up something to help others achieve their dreams and aspirations. They are willing to sacrifice for their loved ones and put themselves last to help them achieve their goals. These selfless acts demonstrate the depth of their love and commitment to each other's happiness and pleasure.

Numerous individuals have been acquainted with narratives recounting instances where they have deferred their endeavors to aid a family member or friend experiencing illness or bereavement. These individuals have consistently exhibited remarkable loyalty and generosity through their aid provision, attentive listening to concerns, and offering encouragement and solace. The generous nature of their actions serves as a prime example of the exceptional lengths we go to secure the well-being and contentment of our loved ones.

These narratives function as a subtle prompt that love encompasses more than fleeting sentiments. Making the happiness of our loved ones a top priority necessitates making sacrifices. We must prioritize our partner's requirements and desires over our own to achieve this objective.

Understanding why and how people put their partners' needs above their own in romantic relationships can lead to self-reflection. They motivate us to examine our dedication and the variety of ways we can show our love for one another because of these people.

Proof of love's transformative power can be found in the many accounts of people who have given up much to care for those they love. They're an eye-catching visual reminder that love isn't just a feeling but a serious commitment that requires giving and receiving. Fostering selflessness, compassion, and lasting affection requires first acknowledging and then recognizing the significance of these efforts.

We talk about setting priorities, stressing the need for a healthy equilibrium between individuals and society's needs. Keep in mind that the happiness and fulfillment of both partners are essential to the health and growth of the relationship.

We must identify our specific requirements and set reasonable boundaries to balance our joint activity's needs and well-being. It is essential to schedule time for introspection, assessment, and revitalization. Good self-care practices help people become better people overall.

Communication is vital for maintaining that delicate balance. Being open and honest with our partner about our needs, desires, and boundaries can aid in developing a solid tie built on trust and security. We may both learn what the other person needs and how to address those needs by discussing the matter thoroughly.

It is also critical to establish defined boundaries. Setting healthy limits in a relationship requires determining what is most important to you and conveying that to your spouse. Taking care of oneself, having one's hobbies and interests, and having one's own space are all examples.

Your participation and effort are critical to the connection. It takes intentional effort to set aside quality time to connect over shared interests, exhibit and receive affection, and enjoy each other's company. The time and effort invested in a connection strengthens it and fosters a shared sense of purpose.

Finding a balance between the needs of relationships and the needs of the individual necessitates constant examination and development. It's a fluid process that evolves as both partners change and grow. When both partners practice appropriate self-care and invest the time and effort required to develop a healthy relationship via open communication, delineated boundaries, and mutual respect, they can fulfill their full potential as individuals and as a pair.

Putting the connection first, however, does not imply ignoring one's own needs or interests. A balancing act entails learning how to care for oneself and one's partner.

Self-care is an essential consideration in love relationships. It is critical to prioritize one's health and pleasure on all levels. Making time for the things that make us happy, creating a regular meditation or mindfulness practice, asking for help when needed, and having clear boundaries can all help us bring our best selves to a relationship.

Identity and the liberty to follow one's interests are also vital considerations. It is critical to continue to develop as a person while simultaneously being a dedicated spouse. Each of us contributes to the depth and vitality of the relationship by following our interests, improving ourselves, and pursuing our goals and dreams.

Communication and mutual understanding are required to balance individual and marital needs. Communicating our thoughts, feelings, and desires to our partners is critical. We should also actively listen to them and try to comprehend their point of view. Both partners can convey their needs and, as a result, receive the support and consideration they require.

Furthermore, it is feasible to prioritize the relationship while still preserving a sense of self by establishing shared interests and hobbies that meet both people's wants and goals. Couples can grow closer and discover shared meaning by engaging in fun activities, making memories, and interacting.

Prioritizing the partnership while still caring for ourselves necessitates finding a happy medium that benefits both sides. We must work hard to assess our circumstances, maintain open lines of communication, and make decisions that are in the best interests of us and the partnership. This strategy provides both parties with a beneficial environment for growth and success.

Retaining healthy boundaries in a relationship is as vital as caring for yourself and keeping your identity. Boundaries preserve our personal needs, values, and space while allowing us to have a secure and loving relationship with our partners. It entails respecting our partner's boundaries while remaining open and honest about our needs, goals, and requirements. The partnership will feel more secure, respectful, and balanced if clear limits are established and enforced.

Putting the connection first requires being present and always paying attention to one another. It entails making an effort to spend time with one another in a leisurely and comfortable manner. We may build our link and develop a more personal relationship by paying complete attention to each other and actively participating in the conversation. This can be accomplished by doing activities together, having in-depth conversations, or simply being there with one another.

It is also essential to have a considerate and understanding point of view. Empathy allows us to understand another person's ideas, feelings, and experiences by putting ourselves in their shoes. It entails showing compassion and support and acknowledging and accepting their feelings and points of view. Empathy is the key to a healthy relationship because it establishes a foundation of safety, trust, and support for both partners.

Finally, it is critical to evaluate our priorities regularly, both as individuals and as a society. Because of the fluid nature of life, our needs and priorities may shift over time. We may ensure that our behaviors and decisions are compatible with our actual objectives and aspirations if we periodically assess our values, goals, and the direction we want our relationship to take. Because we continually reflect on ourselves and learn new things, our relationship is better suited to survive life's inevitable ups and downs.

Self-care, communication, limits, presence, empathy, and regular review are essential for prioritizing the relationship while taking care of ourselves. It necessitates personal development, well-being, and a solid and loving relationship with one's partner. We can have a successful relationship if we work hard in both areas.

Engaging in concessions for one's partner can significantly enhance the strength of a relationship. By prioritizing the desires and pleasures of our partner above our own, we exhibit conspicuous manifestations of selflessness, dedication, and love. The act of making sacrifices within a relationship indicates the mutual commitment and concern shown by both partners toward the prosperity of the relationship.

These acts of selflessness contribute to developing mutual respect and trust within interpersonal relationships. When both individuals involved in a romantic partnership demonstrate a willingness to sacrifice certain aspects of their desires or preferences to prioritize their partner's happiness, it becomes evident that they hold high regard for one another. The awareness of an individual willing to surpass expectations on our behalf instills a sense of grit and assurance within us.

The act of making sacrifices for one another enhances the bond between partners. The willingness to make sacrifices can engender grit and tenacity in facing challenges or impediments. This exemplifies the team's unwavering resolve to surmount obstacles and readiness to make sacrifices to pursue their goals. The strength of your partnership is enhanced through the collective commitment and shared objectives that both parties possess.

Learning to make sacrifices for one another cultivates a deep comprehension and empathy. When individuals empathize with their partners and proactively strive to understand and fulfill their needs and desires, they are more likely to engage in meaningful self-sacrifice. This nature's manifestation of empathy and concern enhances interpersonal connections and emotional closeness among individuals.

Engaging in mutual concessions has the potential to yield a mutually beneficial outcome for all parties involved. When there is a mutual willingness to compromise, a partnership can foster an environment characterized by increased respect and appreciation. Every instance of selflessness presents a valuable occasion to enhance interpersonal connections and deepen mutual understanding. The presence of a positive feedback loop serves to strengthen familial relationships and instill a sense of worth in individuals.

Sacrificing one's desires or needs for the benefit of the other is a strategy that can enhance the bond between individuals in a romantic partnership: trust, resiliency, empathy, and reciprocity experience augmentation. Acts of love, devotion, and selflessness can be exemplified by prioritizing the needs of our spouse and making sacrifices for the betterment of the relationship. The actions of benevolence contribute to the establishment of strong interpersonal connections and serve as a foundation for a lasting and gratifying marital relationship.

Sacrificing something for one's partner also fortifies the interpersonal connection. The act of relinquishing something demonstrates our dedication to the collective group. When individuals acknowledge their collective interconnectedness, they are more inclined to foster an environment of support and motivation among their peers. Creating an environment characterized by respect and admiration can be achieved by prioritizing our partner's needs o

ver our own.

Our willingness to make sacrifices for each other can facilitate both personal growth and the development of our partnership. As mentioned, the phenomenon compels individuals to transcend their customary behavioral patterns and confront novel obstacles to foster interpersonal bonds. The act of sacrifice imparts valuable lessons in tolerance, adaptation, and altruism. These factors enhance our interpersonal bond and facilitate personal development and progress simultaneously.

Sacrificing something for the betterment of another individual is a profound manifestation of affection. The phrase mentioned above is significant beyond mere linguistic expression, as it assumes a tangible representation that serves as a testament to our unwavering dedication to fostering a prosperous alliance. Selfless actions, such as providing time, money, and other types of support to people we care about, are an excellent way to show how much we value them and want them to be happy.

Both sides must show negotiation willingness if they hope to reach agreements that benefit themselves and the other. To achieve this goal, both parties must communicate openly and honestly while respecting one another's privacy and space. When both people in a relationship feel heard and respected, they are more likely to speak their minds openly and honestly with one another. This makes it easier for people to communicate their wants and show they are invested in developing the relationship.

Helping others without expecting anything is a powerful method of building rapport. If this happens, people are likelier to be truthful, work together, advance themselves and others, and care for those around them. By putting our friend's needs ahead of our own, we may build a strong friendship that is good for both of us. Through reinforcing compassion, facilitating selfless activities, and advancing the group through coordinated efforts, the act of sacrifice promotes interpersonal intimacy.

Sacrificing for one another can strengthen relationships and encourage deeper emotional intimacy. To prioritize the needs and desires of others over our own, it is imperative to cultivate a high level of trust and demonstrate a willingness to be vulnerable and receptive. This observation indicates a consistent desire to undertake necessary measures to prioritize the well-being and security of our esteemed individuals. When a significant portion of an individual's emotional and cognitive self-perception becomes intertwined with a romantic partnership, the relationship may evolve into a secure environment wherein both parties can seek solace and achieve dynamic equilibrium.

Engaging in modifications within a relationship can elicit feelings of increased gratitude and appreciation. The extent to which we value the love and dedication of our partners is directly correlated with the level of their contributions toward our well-being. Upon recognizing the significance of the sacrifices made by others on our behalf, we develop a profound gratitude for their actions. We are motivated to express our appreciation for their steadfast commitment. Engaging in acts of gratitude and kindness within a romantic relationship facilitates an emotional connection and establishes a pattern of reciprocal behavior that mutually benefits both individuals involved.

The act of mutual sacrifice can elicit inspiration and motivation among individuals in a constructive manner. The tangible impact of our efforts on the lives of our partners can serve as a motivating force, compelling us to persist and strive for more significant achievements. Upon recognizing our actions' substantial impact on our partner's life, a heightened sense of commitment to the relationship may ensue, fostering increased emotional intimacy with our partner.

When accommodating the needs of a friend, it is crucial to consider that individuals should not compromise their objectives or desires. When individuals mutually benefit from engaging in charitable acts towards one another, it enhances the strength of their interpersonal bond. Effective communication characterized by openness and honesty is imperative for individuals to achieve a mutually satisfactory consensus.

Ultimately, the willingness of a couple to make sacrifices for one another can result in significant individual development for both parties involved. Individuals who undergo this phenomenon exhibit a heightened level of emotional attachment and gratitude, which motivates them to exert maximum effort in their endeavors. Establishing a robust basis for our interpersonal connections becomes more feasible when we demonstrate affection, admiration, and assistance toward our significant others. Acts of benevolence and selflessness serve to fortify the foundation in question. Collaborative efforts are instrumental in attaining both success and happiness. However, it is imperative to prioritize interpersonal connections while simultaneously attending to personal welfare.

Couples can cultivate robust interpersonal bonds by ensuring equitable distribution of household responsibilities and prioritizing individual self-care. In a committed relationship, both individuals must understand and exhibit reverence for their boundaries and those of their significant other. To effectively achieve this objective, both parties must be willing to engage in open and honest dialogue regarding their respective requirements, desires, and boundaries.

Open and honest communication helps couples overcome marital challenges because it fosters respect and understanding. Teams can collaborate to decide on a fair and equal division of household responsibilities by carefully considering one another's wants and concerns. This equitable division reduces tension and hostility by fostering a sense of shared accountability and cooperation.

Both parties must place their needs first for a relationship to flourish last. In a strong relationship, each partner prioritizes their happiness and well-being. People can revitalize themselves and keep their sense of self by engaging in self-care activities, including exercise, hobbies, and relaxation. This helps the person improve their understanding of well-being and fulfillment and affects how they connect with others by increasing their emotional openness, resiliency, and assurance.

Spending time together frequently is also essential to keep the passion fresh and the flames burning. The intentional scheduling of time for bonding activities, conversations, and shared experiences can strengthen and emotionally link a couple's relationship. The relationship between lovers is supported by this conscious attempt to increase the lovers' feelings of love, affection, and closeness.

Couples can eventually develop a relationship based on respect, understanding, and growth if they establish an adequate distribution of home responsibilities and prioritize each person's self-care. Open communication, attentive listening, and intentional engagement help couples overcome their relationship's challenges and create a strong and permanent bond. Happiness, fulfillment, and a thriving love develop when partners treat their needs and the relationships equally.

People who are physically and mentally healthy and have a caring attitude can share sacrifices fairly in a partnership. Each person brings something different to the group effort and is willing to compromise to help the group work better. The level of mutual understanding and friendliness is a sign of enduring loyalty.

In addition, the ability to prioritize the relationship while simultaneously attending to one's own needs requires the presence of self-awareness and the practice of self-care. It is imperative for individuals involved in a relationship to prioritize their personal physical, mental, and emotional well-being through engagement in activities that bring them joy and satisfaction. Self-care enhances an individual's capacity to participate in and provide assistance to a collaborative relationship actively.

It is a never-ending process to put effort into pursuing one's contentment and maintaining healthy connections with others. There must be constant back-and-forth conversation, introspection, and course adjusting. In the long run, couples prioritizing developing their relationship and fulfilling their requirements will likely report persistent pleasure, growth, and gratification.

In basic terms, one partner must accord precedence to the other while simultaneously responding to their particular needs to maintain a mutually gratifying partnership focused on both parties' well-being. To cultivate a healthy relationship, it is essential to display a willingness to compromise, adequately explain one's emotions to one's partner, and actively listen. These three behaviors will help ensure that the relationship thrives. When one member of a pair makes an effort to look after themselves and makes investments in the health of their companion, the relationship between the two people has the potential to endure for a long time.

Chapter 6: The Changing Nature of Love

Love is a compelling energy that has the power to affect both individual livethe lives of people in loves and the whole civilizations ultimately. Throughout my travels, I have observed love's ability to transform lives. It breaks down artificial barriers and creates genuine connections between people from various backgrounds.

Love can transform us and make us better people because of the spark it ignites inside us. It inspires compassion, love, and forgiveness, all of which assist in strengthening our bonds with one another. Love pushes us out of our comfort zones to interact with less fortunate people and provide a helpful hand.

Regarding interpersonal relationships, love can influence people in unforeseen ways. It can mend broken relationships, heal wounded emotions, and restore humanity's hope. Love's precepts include accepting one's and others' flaws, forgiving one another, and letting go of grudges. It allows us to be vulnerable with one another, grow as a community, and progress.

However, the consequences of love extend well beyond human ties. It has the potential to have a positive transformative influence on whole communities. When love permeates society, it fosters an atmosphere of solidarity and collaboration. People put aside their differences and collaborate to achieve a common objective. Because of the love they get, empathy grows, and people are inspired to find ways to help and uplift others.

People are likely to speak out against injustice, bigotry, and oppression in cultures where love is strongly valued. Love inspires people to act, promoting open communication and a more inclusive community. It motivates us to question conventions and work for a more just and equitable society.

Prejudices and obstacles can also be overcome via love. It allows us to see past superficial differences and appreciate each person for who they are at their heart. We can accept people for who they are through love, and we can understand the variety that each person provides to our lives.

When commence commencing on a romantic adventure, we must comprehend the transformational power of love. It motivates us to share love and inspire others to be the change we want to see in the world. If love is the ultimate incentive for our decisions and actionsSuppose love is the ultimate incentive for our decisions and actions. In that case, we will have a more compassionate, welcoming, and peaceful society.

Love has great transformational power. It can heal even the most severe wounds, mend even the most strained of bonds, and reunite those who have drifted apart. Throughout my travels, I have observed love's extraordinary power to transform people and whole communities.

Love has a significant effect on individuals. It can encourage us to look beyond our current circumstances and focus on our strengths. When one is in love, one feels respected, protected, and understood. It gives us the willpower to follow our goals, overcome anxieties, and evolve. We have an impact on individuals in our sphere of influence because we are motivated by love to better ourselves.

Love can change our views of closeness, trust, and connection in romantic relationships. It drives us to give aside our desires in favor of the satisfaction of our partners. To sustain harmony, love teaches us the importance of open communication, attentive listening, and a little bit of giving. It helps us create safe surroundings for love to develop, resulting in ties resisting anything.

On the other hand, love's effects go far beyond people and groups. They reach across whole cultures. Acceptance, respect, and working together grow in a caring place. It gets people talking and ensures that all points of view are considered. When motivated by love, people put aside their differences and work together to reach shared goals. This is good for the community as a whole.

People who care about each other help those who are in trouble. When people are touched by love, they are more likely to help those in need. It motivates people to work together to fight against social injustice, protect the environment, and make their neighborhoods better. The power of love, which moves people at all levels of society to act, could be the spark for a more fair and open community.

Love has the power to question and change the rules of society. It deals directly with problems of discrimination. When we fall in love, it shakes our ideas about the world and helps us see it more complexly. It gives us the strength to stand up for the weak and ask for justice. A loving society honors that people have different ideas and values them all the same.

Since love changes, it's essential to be aware of the problems that could come up in a relationship. When done with courage and drive, looking for love can be an exciting and, in the end, gratifying journey. Everyone must learn to take credit for their work and work hard to improve. Setting up ways to talk to each other, practicing forgiveness, and letting go of old grudges are all things that could help. Love is complicated, but it always makes people happy and whole.

The undeniable capacity of love to bring about positive transformation in individuals and communities is a subject of great significance. The well-being of individuals, relationships, and communities is enhanced when individuals exhibit receptiveness toward receiving love. The enhancement of our capacity for compassion and understanding is imperative. Acknowledging the fluidity of love and responding appropriately could have significant implications. Let us endeavor to create a global society in which love is the primary motivator for our interactions and behaviors toward each other. However, love is a potent sentiment that can yield extraordinary outcomes.

The love I have experienced has played a significant role in shaping my personal development and contributing to my overall sense of life fulfillment. The personal growth resulting from this experience has led to enhanced emotional resilience and a broader perspective on the world. Articulating the profound influence that love has exerted on my life proves to be a challenging task.

The capacity of an individual to cultivate and actualize their complete capabilities is augmented when they experience a sense of affection and care. Experiencing care and acceptance from my closest companions has consistently instilled a sense of security and value. As a result of the conducive and agreeable environment, I experienced a heightened sense of agency and control over my life. This experience has sparked my interest in self-exploration and personal development. Based on my experiences, it is evident that perceiving one's strengths and weaknesses within the framework of love can foster greater self-acceptance.

The acquisition of knowledge regarding compassion and empathy through love experiences has significantly influenced my perspective on life. This experience has facilitated effective intercultural communication with individuals from diverse cultural backgrounds. The enhancement of my interpersonal relationships can be attributed to the development of my heightened sensitivity and compassion through the experience of love. The experiences pertaining to love have imparted upon me the understanding of every individual's intrinsic significance and merit based on their inherent qualities and characteristics. This experience has provided valuable insights into enhancing my interpersonal interactions more constructively.

Love has been pivotal in my quest for personal satisfaction, and its magnitude cannot be overstated. The critical insight derived from this experience is that individuals in my social circle hold significantly more significant importance to me compared to material wealth or public recognition. Undoubtedly, the affection bestowed upon me by my marital partner has profoundly impacted the trajectory of my existence. The development of regular routines, the cultivation of gratitude towards individuals in my social circle, and the recognition of the significance inherent in everyday activities have all assumed greater importance in my life due to this experience.

Love has always been an essential source of strength in the face of adversity throughout history. The utilization of this particular resource has proven to be effective in alleviating emotional distress and apprehension experienced during periods of grief and adversity. Love has imparted upon me a profound understanding of the extent to which I am cherished and the measures individuals are willing to undertake to secure their gratification. Believing in the enduring power of love to provide sustenance and guidance during times of hardship enables me to confront and overcome the various obstacles encountered in life.

The concept of love has played a crucial role in my personal development and overall well-being. This opportunity has allowed me to engage with individuals of great interest and recognize the significance of cultivating patience and empathy. A consistent association exists between love, enhanced mental well-being, and the ability to cope with challenging circumstances. The impact of love on my life has expedited my journey toward personal satisfaction and achievement, for which I am immensely grateful.

The experience of love, in addition to my interactions with others, is a major factor in my development and happiness. As a consequence of this, my perception of both the world and myself has undergone a significant transformation. As a result of experiencing love, I have acquired the ability to cultivate an appreciation for life's subtleties and perceive any situation's positive aspects.

Throughout my personal development, I have recognized the significance of self-esteem and self-nurturing. This particular experience has given me insight into the importance of prioritizing one's unique needs over the needs of others. When individuals strongly believe in their values, they prioritize their overall well-being. This experience has given me valuable insights into boundaries, emphasizing the importance of prioritizing my well-being and engaging in activities that enhance my overall quality of life. After experiencing the consequences of my actions, I have prioritized my happiness as a primary consideration in romantic relationships. To cultivate mutually beneficial relationships with individuals, it is imperative to prioritize self-care.

The experience of love has also influenced my reaction to challenging circumstances. This could provide me with fortitude during periods of hardship. The author's positive perspective and inner strength have been significantly influenced by the knowledge gained and behaviors adopted through interpersonal experiences, particularly those rooted in affection and emotional bonding. With an enhanced sense of self-assurance, I am confident in my aptitude, ensuring my future success. The experience of having experienced love has provided me with the inner calm and resilience necessary to navigate the unavoidable challenges that arise in life.

The experience of love has additionally broadened and imbued my heart with tenderness. The knowledge I have acquired from this experience highlights the significance of prioritizing the needs of others over my own. Based on my personal experiences, it has become evident that investing effort in providing encouragement and facilitating the endeavors of others in their quest for happiness yields significant value. I am motivated to offer assistance due to my experience witnessing the profound impact of love.

The experience of love has broadened my perspective, allowing me to perceive the inherent interconnectedness within all life forms. The knowledge acquired from this experience suggests that individuals possess the capacity to effect change on a global scale. This experience has motivated me to extend my assistance towards initiatives that advocate for facilitating inter-community dialogue and collaboration. Through personal experiences, I have understood that love can catalyze positive change in societysocietal change. It has imparted upon me the realization that I can make a meaningful difference in the world by courageously championing moral principles and actively advocating for the well-being and contentment of individuals in my vicinity.

The concept of love has played a significant role in shaping my personal growth and overall satisfaction. As a result of this experience, I have undergone a transformative process, leading to a heightened sense of personal identity characterized by increased emotional range and enhanced complexity of character. My personal development has been significantly shaped by the individuals I hold dear. I was instructed on the importance of prioritizing personal happiness, resolving challenges, and making meaningful contributions to society at large. The acquisition of knowledge regarding the requisites for achieving success in life has been greatly facilitated by exploring the concept of love. This exploration has revealed the significance of expending diligent effort in cultivating favorable interpersonal relationships, prioritizing personal gratification, and genuinely demonstrating concern for the welfare of others in one's immediate vicinity.

I recently engaged in a conversationconversed with an individual whose romantic relationship significantly impacted their personal growth and development. Various challenges have emerged throughout this research topic's existence but have consistently been resolved. However, a significant and permanent transformation occurred after an encounter establishing a romantic connection of unparalleled depth. The individuals exhibited high trust in one another and entered into a lifelong commitment.

Due to their reciprocal fondness, they were able to motivate themselves to strive for more significant achievements. The occurrence imbued within them an intense resolve that propelled their progress and furnished them with the necessary skills to navigate comparable circumstances in subsequent instances. The group's primary objective was to abstain from detrimental influences and strive for personal improvement, serving as a motivating factor.

During one of my expeditions, I encountered an individual whose existence had undergone a profound transformation due to the influence of love. Due to their perceived isolation, the individual experienced deep feelings of loneliness. However, as their emotional attachment to each other intensified, a significant transformation occurred.

Because of this, people felt like they belonged, were known, and were part of a group. Because of this, most people felt better and more satisfied with their lives. Because of this, kids learn to value relationships with other people and care about their peers. There was an apparent rise in people's willingness to help and be kind, and they worked hard to improve the lives of people in their local area.

Someone I know had a lot of anger, dislike, and hatred for a long time. The person's mental health was worsening because they had already been hurt and lost a lot. Still, falling in love changed their lives for good.

People could let go of their anger and forgive themselves because of this powerful feeling. People learned more about themselves and how to forgive those who hurt them. As a result of their newfound love, people's hearts were healed, and their ideas about what makes them happy grew. The power of love can improve a person's mental health and help them learn to be more compassionate and understanding.

I once met someone who seemed very confused and whose life was going in no particular direction. Still, love changed everything when it was brought into the world. Both of the people in this relationship thought they could do anything.
The people were driven to reach their goals, and they believed they could make a change in the world. Even when they thought they were in trouble, their love for each other kept them going. Their deep love for each other gave them a lot of happiness and a sense of direction in life. The people's experiences with love have changed them profoundly, and because of this, they want to make the world a better place.

All of the stories here are about how falling in love changed the main character's life in a big way. This led to, among other things, self-reflection, growth, doing valuable items, and stronger social ties. The fact that these people's lives changed so much because of their relationships shows that love can change things.

Forgiving and helping others has helped me immensely with self-compassion and personal growth. Before I got over my hurt and anger, I couldn't understand why it was necessary to forgive others. After learning to control my bad feelings, I finally understood and accepted the idea of love.

As I got better at forgetting things, my ability to feel understanding and kindness grew. Being kind to others can improve their lives, and it might and even help them find love. Having empathy makes it easier to accept that other people are human and have flaws.

After learning to accept and show kindness, my heart feels love better. The study found a link between being kind and helpful to others and getting more love in return. People were more thoughtful and forgiving after a run of good things got started. This made it easier for people to get to know each other and gave people in the community a feeling of belonging and kindness.

Moreover, the act of demonstrating kindness and forgiveness towards others played a pivotal role in facilitating the process of healing deep-seated emotional traumas that I had been harboring for an extended duration. Consequently, I demonstrated self-compassion and identified areas in which I needed improvement. It is comprehended that extending forgiveness to others can facilitate self-forgiveness, as it acknowledges the shared humanity among individuals and the inherent entitlement to opportunities for redemption. Through the process of self-acceptance, I experienced an improvement in my self-perception and an enhanced capacity to cultivate love and compassion toward others.

The practice of compassion and forgiveness has transformed my path to love. They showed me how forgiveness and acceptance may increase one's capacity for love. I have built love not just in my relationships with others but also in my relationships with myself through acts of forgiveness and compassion. I can cultivate an eternally evolving love by forgiving people and being friendly.

I've noticed that the more I can forgive and offer compassion, the deeper and broader my love develops. Forgiveness is an essential first step on the journey to compassion and understanding. My propensity to keep grudges has severely limited my ability to love and be loved.

I make room for reconciliation and peace by extending grace to those who have offended me. As a result of letting go of my attachment to the past, I can now genuinely enjoy the present. Because of forgiveness, I can repair trust and develop a feeling of community and peace. It's a moving illustration of how love can mend broken things.

My kindness practice has substantially boosted my emotional maturity. I exhibit sympathy because I see that, despite their suffering, the other person retains humanity. Consequently, I can see past little differences and form profound bonds with people. Because I can empathize with others, I can be a helpful friend and a secure environment for individuals to open up. These acts of kindness build my connections with others and give me a feeling of purpose in life.

My life has dramatically improved due to forgiving others and demonstrating compassion. My ability to release fury, bitterness, and criticism has grown. I may let go of the past and embrace a brighter, more loving future by ignoring it. Kindness to others not only benefits them but also makes me happy. It's a good reminder of how interconnected we are and how helpful conversations can be.

I've realized that love is a discipline along this path of kindness and compassion. It necessitates the ability to forgive past wrongs and be tolerant and sympathetic. With each act of kindness and excellent action, I perform, I am cultivating a love that increases in depth and breadth.

Subsequently, getting better at being kind and forgiving has been very important to the health of my relationship. It has helped me heal emotionally, have more meaningful relationships with other people, and build understanding and kindness. When I forgive, I am freed from anger, and empathy lets me connect fully with others. As I work on forgiving and being kind, I'm aware of how love can change my life and the lives of those around me.

If love is widely shared, it has the potential to change the world for the better. I saw the positive effects of giving love and doing pleasant things personally. Love breaks through walls and motivates others to do the same, setting off a chain reaction of good actions.

I've experienced firsthand how spreading love may offer joy to hurting others. People might always benefit from more compassion, a listening ear, or a genuine smile. In despair, love can give a light of hope and solidarity to those around you.

Sharing love develops a sense of belonging and camaraderie. It allows for contact and mutual learning among people with diverse identities, cultures, and worldviews. We should value and cherish our shared humanity, and love teaches us how. As a consequence, everyone feels appreciated, respected, and included.

Love can change entire societies and has an influence far beyond our connections. Sharing love inspires people to work together for a brighter future. People inspired by love are more likely to speak out against injustice, strive for social justice, and improve the happiness of all. It motivates us to band together and work together to build a more peaceful and welcoming global society.

Also, liking other people has a significant good effect on our health. We show respect, kindness, and hope when we choose to be nice to others. It changes how we see the world and makes us more aware of how kind and beautiful it is. By focusing on love, we become agents of change who can help build a more loving and caring world.

The dissemination of love has a massive ripple effect. It has the potential to bring people together, foster togetherness, and inspire constructive action. We may set off a chain reaction that benefits many others by assisting others. We not only brighten the lives of others around us by being brilliant examples of love, compassion, and hope, but we also go through a profound personal metamorphosis.

We may inspire people to be kind and compassionate to one another by being kind and compassionate to one another. Love can cross borders and affect people in unforeseen ways. It's an unstoppable force that can enhance things on all levels, from the individual to the collective.

Compassionate conduct transforms us to become change agents. Even the smallest gesture of love may have a significant impact. Others may be encouraged to help others due to your kind heart. It sets off a chain reaction that affects the lives of people we'll never meet.

Spreading love can heal and restore. Those who want consolation may find agonizing relief in the embrace of love. They take peace in knowing they are not alone and others have had similar experiences. With love, we create a secure atmosphere where people may recover from trauma and develop more robust.

Sharing love also can break down barriers and make people respect each other more. Love can bring together people who would never get along because of their differences. It can also help people feel love and understand each other in a world where division is all too familiar. When we look past people's noticeable differences and treat them respectfully, we create a place where everyone feels respected and at home. We can put aside our disagreements and talk to each other about important things because of the power of love.

Also, if you treat them well, they are likely towill likely do the same for you. Giving love to other people makes us feel better about ourselves. When we show love to others, we feel like our lives have a point. It makes us more excited about the possibility of improving people's lives and more aware of our power to do so.

Those who promote love have the potential to change the world. It's an excellent way to encourage health, community, and empathy. Acts of kindness and compassion result in a better, more compassionate society. Let us use our potential to share love to make the world a more loving and caring place. This will establish a loving legacy that will outlast our lifetimes.

Sharing love can solve more significant societal concerns in addition to its sound effects on people and communities. Love has the potential to be a strong force in the fight for social justice, equality, and inclusion. By being pleasant to others, we may combat prejudice, remove societal barriers, and work toward a society where everyone is treated with dignity.

Apart fromBesides its beneficial impact on individuals and communities, love can induce transformative shifts in attitudes and beliefs, thereby offering a promising avenue for tackling significant societal issues. Love as a catalyst can enhance societal aspects such as social justice, equality, and inclusivity, provided it is actively advocated for and disseminated within the community.

Love is a powerful tool in reducing racism because it can cultivate empathy and promote mutual comprehension. When individuals are treated with love and compassion, it fosters personal and collective growth. Demonstrating such benevolence makes it plausible that the detrimental effects of prejudice stemming from misinterpretation and lack of confidence can be surmounted. When individuals engage in active listening, they acquire the ability to cultivate empathy toward others and overcome the inherent biases that perpetuate prejudice.

Love has the potential to dismantle societal barriers and foster greater openness within a community. Adopting the principle of love as our guiding framework will facilitate our efforts to challenge the systemic regulations that perpetuate

126

social inequities and restrict specific individuals to their current circumstances. To uphold the principles of love, it is imperative to safeguard all individuals' equal entitlements and prospects, irrespective of their race, gender, sexual orientation, or socioeconomic circumstances. This statement motivates us to actively confront the underlying factors contributing to social inequality and dismantle the various obstacles that hinder individuals from realizing their complete capabilities within our societal framework.

In a society where love is the primary motivator, individuals are more inclined to address and mitigate instances of bias and injustice actively. In the presence of injustice, the presence of love fortifies our determination to pursue social justice and foster a state of equilibrium. The virtues of kindness and consideration towards one another play a pivotal role in fostering a societal framework that acknowledges and values the contributions made by all individuals.

Let us collectively unite in pursuit of love. Due to the interconnectedness fostered by affection, we can effectuate positive transformations globally, thereby ensuring their enduring impact. The potency of love enables collective efforts to tackle societal obstacles that may otherwise seem insurmountable. The emotion of love facilitates our ability to engage in collaborative efforts to construct a society characterized by principles of fairness, equality, and inclusivity.

Within advocating for social justice, equality, and inclusion, it is worth acknowledging that love can exert a significant and influential impact. Utilizing love in interpersonal interactions is a potent strategy for reducing prejudice, dismantling constructed divisions, and advancing the pursuit of a more equitable and impartial global society. The potency of affection has the potential to motivate individuals to take up arms and advocate for a more promising tomorrow, thereby cultivating a culture characterized by heightened empathy, goodness, and peace.

By promoting love, wPromoting love may impact change in a world where hate and division are prevalent. When the force of love wins over negativity, disagreements may become chances to learn more about one another. It improves communication and builds interpersonal ties. By practicing kindness, we may build communities where individuals feel included, heard, and ready to make a difference.

Being kind and considerate to other peoples is rewarding in more ways than one, and those rewards continue to accrue even after the original recipients have been assisted. When we behave and engage with other peoples with love, we motivate others around us to do the same. It grows into a large social movement that has implications in a variety of different areas of society. Generosity and thoughtfulness spread like wildfire whenever one personsomeone does something kind for another person. The beneficial impacts of love may have this kind of multiplied effect, which in turn can have an influence oninfluence the collective consciousness.

It is beneficial to society as a whole, as well as to the health and satisfaction of individual people, and to the health and satisfaction of individual people to spread love. Bringing happiness to the lives of others via acts of compassion and love also has a positive effect on our own life. The feeling of purpose, belonging, and accomplishment are all enhanced by love. As a direct result of this, there is a greater feeling of community and of helping one another. We have the ability tocan make the world a better and more enjoyable place to live by practicing acts of thoughtfulness and kindness.

Exchanging love has been shown to have positive effects onpositively affect both the physical and emotional well-being of partnerersons. According to the findings of a scientific study, compassion, and love trigger the creation of endorphins and other "feel-good" molecules in the body. These chemicals are advantageous to our demeanor as well as our overall mental and physical wellness.

Being compassionate toward others has a multiplicative effect on our own level of pleasure. Our capacity for kindness and charity grows in direct proportion to the frequency and intensity with which we participate in acts of beneficence benevolence and understanding. In turn, tThis strengthens our emotional resilience and helps us cultivate a sense of inner happiness and serenity.

Affectionate exchanges also help to cultivate a feeling of community and belonging. The fact that we are all related to one another is brought to our attention by this. People who admire others tend to acquire greater compassion and empathy, which enables them to overcome prejudice and function more effectively in the workplace.

An affectionate expression may also serve as a source of motivation for others around you. It's possible that the decisions we make will encourage and inspire people around us. When we act kindly and compassionately on a regular basis, it inspires people around us to do the same, which in turn creates a positive feedback loop that continues to grow.

In the long run, increasing the amount of love that exists in the world is beneficial not just to the psychological and physiological health of people but also to the health of society as a whole. When we are generous and kind to other people, we not only make their lives better but also make our own lives better in the process. Love enhances not only the relationships between people but also their feeling of purpose and their sense of belonging in the world of belonging. Let's work together to establish a society where loving-kindness and compassion are the norm by first having faith in the transformational power of love and then working together to bring that belief to fruition. Together, we have the power to make the world a better place by making it healthier, happier, and more nurturing.

Chapter 7: Leaving a Love Legacy

The idea of leaving a Love Legacy is very important and life-changing because it's about making a positive and lasting change in other people's lives through acts of kindness and love. Building strong relationships with the people we live with is more important than getting rich or having short-term success. A Love Legacy shows compassion, understanding, and respect to everyone we meet, whether friends, family members, or strangers. We may profoundly impact their lives and make a lasting mark on their hearts if we fill our encounters with love and compassion. Long after we are gone, the love and compassion we have left behind will motivate others to continue the excellent work we began. Because it is timeless and universal, a Love Legacy significantly influences the Earth and everyone who lives on it.

A Love Legacy's power may reach well beyond our local circle of influence; it recognizes no limits of geography or class. Our actions of kindness and optimism can have a ripple effect on individuals we will never meet. A legacy is produced when the love we plant today grows and flourishes in the hearts of people we have touched and inspired.

This love may spread like a tsunami, impacting individuals worldwide and bridging cultural differences. When we leave a loving legacy, we help promote tolerance and love worldwide. Positive energy may spread like wildfire when our acts and love touch people's hearts from all walks of life.

One of the most appealing aspects of a love legacy is its ability to last. Love may be shared and experienced in many languages and cultures. It holds the human family together, bridging our differences and joining us.

We may only partially comprehend the impact of the love and compassion we spread. A single act of charity, kindness, or a word of encouragement may have a long-term influence on someone's life. It may help you feel better, forgive people, and preserve hope when circumstances appear grim.

Long after we are gone, the people we have touched with our love will transfer to new locations and allow it to bloom. Our compassion may set off a chain reaction that benefits future generations.

Our loving legacy will act as a constant reminder of what we value. It forms an essential part of our life story, impacting how people remember us throughout time. Our love legacy is a gift to the world that lives on and inspires future generations to follow in our footsteps. We form an eternal bond when we give love and charity to the next generation. Finally, a legacy of love knows no bounds; it encompasses not just ourselves but everyone and everything. It acts as a force that continues accomplishing good things and enhancing the planet. As we work hard to sow seeds of love in the lives of those we touch that will bear fruit long after we are gone, let us consider the impact we will have on the globe when we are gone.

To leave a loving legacy, one must be genuine and selfless. Giving without expecting anything in return, lending a helping hand without expecting anything in return, and assisting those in need are all aspects of being a source of strength and support for others. Being a bright and cheerful light in a dark and often brutal world.

Love's legacy is beautiful not just because of its influence on current and future generations but also because of the enormous joy it offers us today. When we prioritize loving and being polite to others, we discover more significant meaning and happiness in our lives. The warmth from expressing love is its reward, unrivaled in this world.

Every day, we can intentionally choose to leave a legacy of love. It doesn't have to be elaborate; a simple smile, pleasant words, or thoughtful deed may go a long way. Even seemingly insignificant acts of kindness can have a long-term influence and spread goodwill across many people's lives.

A legacy of love is the finest legacy we can leave for our loved ones—an everlasting homage to the strength of love and the human spirit. By leaving a Love Legacy, we can change the world and have a lasting influence long after we have passed away. So, to leave a loving legacy, let us strive to make the world a more loving place.

As we learn more about it, we realize that leaving a loving legacy is timeless and eternal. Love is an unbreakable force that is unstoppable by anything, including death. Having a good effect on other people's life is the finest way to leave a lasting legacy of compassion and empathy.

Love Legacy requires minimal gestures or widespread recognition. It manifests itself in the silent actions of bravery and inspiration that help people in need without drawing attention to themselves. It improves the quality of life for everyone who comes into contact with it. It is a love fabric made up of many actions of giving.

Love Legacy has an impact that extends beyond our immediate family. We welcome every member of the human family. We contribute to forming a more peaceful and compassionate society when we are kind and tolerant to individuals who are different from us in terms of race, religion, gender, sexual orientation, and socioeconomic status.

Leaving a Love Legacy inspires future generations to continue spreading love and compassion. When we illustrate how love can improve a person's life, we sow the seeds of understanding in the minds and hearts of others. Love has a contagious effect that inspires those who come into contact with it to continue the transformation by becoming changemakers themselves. Love Legacy is a powerful antidote to our sometimes chaotic and volatile environment. It's a great example of what people can do when remembering our shared humanity. It serves as a reminder that love is powerful enough to overcome adversity and reunite people who have grown apart.

If we wish to leave a Love Legacy, we must constantly act morally and honestly. It pushes us to be honest with ourselves and behave following our values. When we act from a place of unshakable love, we encourage others to do the same.

Finally, a loving legacy is a sentimental legacy. It provides proof of our generosity and friendliness to one another. We left behind memories to be told, laughter to be shared, and tears to be shed in the understanding that love persists even without physical touch.

Let us remember that our choices, words, and actions all have the power to create a legacy of love. Our contribution to this incredible symphony of love will impact the environment and the lives of individuals whose hearts we touch.

The road to leaving a Love Legacy may be difficult. It's easy to feel sorry for yourself when the people we care about show little interest in us or even apparent hatred against us. When times are harsh, the tenacity of a Love Legacy shows through the most. It's critical to remember that, whatever the odds, actions of compassion and generosity have the potential to develop into something beautiful.

Self-compassion is equally crucial if we want to leave a legacy of kindness. We occasionally fall short of our standards because we are not flawless. On the other hand, accepting our flaws with tolerance and compassion is critical for our personal progress. By increasing our capacity for self-love and self-compassion, we may have more to give to others.

A person who tries to understand and help others without passing judgment is leaving a legacy of love. We may better understand one another and form bonds that respect our shared humanity if we take the time to listen to one another's stories and life experiences.

Love Legacy includes the natural environment, all other life forms on Earth, and people. Protecting the environment and demonstrating love to all living beings, huge or little, are two parts of leaving a Love Legacy for future generations. One method to safeguard the Earth and make it a better place for future generations is to promote sustainable practices and a natural way of life.

As we evaluate its significance, let us analyze the implications of leaving a loving legacy. No matter how small, every act of kindness contributes to a tsunami of benevolence that might sweep the planet. Consider living in a world where compassion, kindness, and love are the unifying factors that hold everyone together.

A Love Legacy is ultimately about who wants to improve the world, not who gets the spotlight. It's about making a lasting impression on future generations' hearts and brains. Everyone can choose how they want to be remembered, and leaving a Love Legacy is always possible.

To leave a loving legacy, you need a generous attitude that puts the impact you can have on other people's lives ahead of your own. It means being driven by a desire to build a society in which all human interactions are based on care, kindness, and love.

A Love Legacy is made up of small acts of kindness and caring done daily that add up to something special. Small acts of kindness, like a smile or a helping hand, can significantly affect and encourage people to keep giving and getting love for a long time.

To leave a Love Legacy, you must make a promise that lasts your whole life, not just for one event. It means staying kind and understanding even when things are hard or people disagree. It's about understanding how different people are and recognizing how our shared situations have made us who we are.

A Love Legacy is appealing partly because it stays with you. Love lasts forever and is shared by everyone. It grows and changes even in the lives of people we may never meet. So, the views and ideals of future generations are altered in a way that will last.

Everyone can leave their mark on the world. By leaving a Love Legacy, they set an excellent example for others and give them hope. They show how love can heal broken hearts, unite people, and make the world kinder.

Even though life can be challenging, it is essential to remember that we can always leave a Love Legacy. It starts with putting relationships ahead of everything else, putting people first, and leading with love and kindness.

What matters is the heritage of love, which changes the course of events and leaves a lasting mark on the minds and hearts of people who come after us. Let's all promise to leave a Love Legacy so that future generations can live in a world where peace, unity, and respect for everyone are the most important things.

Allow me to share the beautiful consequences of kindness and compassion in today's world. The world would be better if more people consciously treated others with kindness, compassion, and generosity.

When we are kind to one another, we set off a chain reaction of compassion that benefits the entire world. Your kind words, little encouragement, or random acts of kindness may make someone's day and lift their spirits. As a result of the power of love, people may take action, starting a chain reaction of good actions that benefits everyone in its path and beyond.

Positive actions that assist others have a cumulative effect on our happiness. Helping others gives us the satisfaction and delight that comes from knowing we have positively impacted someone else's life. It deepens our belief in our shared humanity and gives our existence more meaning.

Spreading compassion and kindness also brings people closer together and to the rest of the globe. It allows individuals of many cultures and religions to interact. It fosters an environment in which people feel valued and cared for.

As we begin our mission to improve the world, remember that even the most straightforward actions may have an influence. Even the most minor acts of kindness, such as being there for a friend when they need us, working for a cause we believe in, or just smiling at someone, may have a tremendous impact.

I'll conclude by encouraging you to join me in making a difference via acts of compassion and love. Let us be the ones to effect good change, aware that even the smallest of our efforts may result in a better society in which everyone can coexist in peace and harmony. We can change the world one deed at a time. Let us make the world a better place for everyone by loving one another and doing good.

Let us begin each day with an open mind and a desire to do good. As we go about our everyday lives, let us be aware of our chances to impact others around us positively. Holding the door open, assisting a neighbor in need, or reaching out to a suffering friend are little acts of kindness.

We can make the world a better place for everyone by helping one another and exhibiting compassion. Being the change we wish to see in the world may encourage others to do the same. Our activities create an excellent example for others by demonstrating the transformative power of compassion and understanding.

Let us not forget that our loving deeds will have an influence even after we have passed away. Those we care for and assist will remember our kindness and compassion for them for the rest of their lives. Even after the conversation, the recipient may be left with a sense of warmth and friendliness.

On a personal level, sharing love and doing pleasant things has a tremendous impact on our level of happiness. It has been demonstrated that being nice to others improves our self-esteem, decreases stress, and boosts our joy and fulfillment. To nurture our souls and give our lives more purpose, we must decide to be a source of love and optimism for others.

So, let us believe in compassion and the ability to care for one another to alter lives. By our behaviors, we may all benefit from a kinder and gentler world. Because assisting others improves their quality of life, it multiplies our happiness. Let us commit to leaving a positive legacy that touches people's hearts and motivates them to act for future generations' sake.

Good deeds do not have to be complicated and may happen at anytime. If you want to improve someone's day, it takes a few minutes to be kind to a stranger, encourage a friend, or perform a little favor for a coworker.

Because they are so simple, anyone can do helpful things. Small acts of kindness can make a big difference in the lives of the people they affect and the world. The more I put the idea of showing love through small acts of kindness into practice, the more I see how it makes the lives of the people around me better and my own.

Even simple things like looking at a stranger on the street, holding the door open for them, or praising them can significantly affect how they feel and what they think about the world. These small things can go a long way toward making someone happy and making them feel like they are loved.

It can help a friend or family member hear words of support and inspiration during hard times. Someone can keep going because of one positive word or sentence. I know how important it is to be there for people, both when they are happy and sad.

Also, if a boss encourages their employees to do small acts of kindness, it can help build peace and happiness. Small acts of kindness, like helping a friend when they need it, giving them a cup of coffee, or telling them how much you appreciate their work, can make a big difference in how people feel at work.

As I do these small acts of kindness every day, I'm becoming more and more sure that everyone has the power to make a change in the lives of those around them. Even on the busiest or most busy days, being nice could make all the difference.

Good things also spread like flames. If we help other people, they are more likely to help others. This chain of good deeds makes our society a kinder and more loving place to live.

Remember to value the importance of empathy. We may attain mutual understanding and reconciliation when we hear and comprehend one another. We may use our hearts to put ourselves in another person's shoes and respond to their needs when they are suffering problems or unhappiness.

Rather than working alone, we should partner with other concerned individuals and groups to address the world's most pressing concerns. When we work together, our love and good acts have a more significant impact. Whether working on community projects, volunteering for a cause, or supporting programs that promote justice and equality, our collective actions might have a huge impact.

It's critical to remember that acts of compassion and love spread far and wide. In today's global climate, a random act of kindness may immediately and profoundly influence people worldwide.

Let us remember the transformational power of love and compassionate acts. Let us bear in mind as we go that what we do affects not just people around us but also ourselves. May our interactions and decisions be guided by our shared desire to help others and promote love. Let us light a fire in the hearts of everyone we come into contact with by spreading our love far and wide.

Implanting caring ideals in the next generation is critical to establish a more compassionate and peaceful society. Looking back on my life, I know how important it is to instill the ideals of love and kindness in the next generation.

When we educate the next generation on how to love, we provide them with the tools they need to establish more robust and rewarding relationships with others. By instilling compassion, open communication, and understanding, we may create a culture where these traits are the norm and problems are settled amicably and respectfully.

Sharing caring teachings also helps to develop a sense of responsibility for one's neighborhood and the more fantastic world. It instills in the next generation a sense of responsibility and the necessity to regard the sentiments of others when acting.

Our efforts to instill compassion and understanding in future generations will be very beneficial. When children grasp the value of self-love and compassion, they are better prepared to face problems and resist peer pressure.

Giving loving lessons to others is one way we respect our forefathers and the events that formed us. Bypassing these principles on, we may ensure that the essence of love and compassion stands the test of time and contributes to the development of the world for future generations.

The transmission of loving lessons to the next generation is the only way to create a more compassionate and understanding society. The traditional wisdom of love and compassion is preserved for future generations delight and emulation while also providing young brains with the talents and concepts required to develop healthy relationships. By disseminating these compassionate principles, we can build a more peaceful and prosperous society that recognizes and honors the transformational power of love.

We hope to inspire the next generation to take the lead in transforming the world by teaching them these humane principles. We encourage kids to take the information to improve the world by demonstrating the far-reaching effects of even the most insignificant acts of kindness.

When compassionate guidance is provided across generations, it strengthens relationships between people of all ages. Everyone may benefit from in-depth discussions and shared information between generations.

The most effective strategy to pass on social skills to the next generation is to instill compassion and love in them. Children who learn to speak with empathy and settle disagreements with understanding will be better equipped to deal with the complexities of adult life and form positive relationships.

Another reason for handing down such ideas is to instill in future generations the value of appreciating the present. It serves as a reminder to respect the people in our lives and work to strengthen the bonds that bind them to us. Long after we are gone, the love seeds we plant in the hearts of future generations will bloom and grow.

Finally, a person may impact the world by teaching their children the value of love. It fosters intergenerational empathy, provides young people with the tools they need to improve the world, and prepares them for maturity. By keeping and cultivating the qualities of love and compassion, we leave a kind legacy that will benefit future generations. Let us happily accept the duty of handing these humanitarian ideas to the next generation, confident that our actions will leave the world a better, more peaceful place.

As we continue to foster the characteristics of kindness and compassion in our children, we must not overlook the importance of leading by example. The generation behind us studies how we treat people and deal with life's issues and draws inspiration from us.

It is critical to foster cultures where generosity and empathy are exercised regularly. We can help people become more socially and emotionally aware by creating surroundings where they are appreciated.

Inspiring youngsters to challenge the current quo and develop their critical thinking abilities is part of teaching them loving lessons. We can inspire a new generation of compassionate activists who will help to improve the world by giving them the resources they need to resist injustice and bring about constructive change.

Let us not avoid frank dialogues about prejudice, inequality, and violence with the next generation. By having honest and open talks, we may help children comprehend the intricacies of the world and equip them to contribute to finding a solution.

And anyone other than parents and teachers might teach their children valuable life lessons. Family, friends, and role models aid the collaborative effort. Future leaders will benefit from the compassion and empathy we can instill in their minds and hearts.

Teaching people to love is a continual effort that requires focus, intention, and consistency. It is about training young people to think about others and cultivating those ideas into long-lasting affection. Assured that our combined efforts will have a long-term influence on the world's future, making it a better, more compassionate place, let us remain steadfast in our commitment to impart these critical teachings. We will leave the world a better place by inspiring the next generation of compassionate changemakers.

By being thoughtful to others and attentive to what they have to say, I hope to make an indelible impression on the world. We may develop relationships with individuals that make us more sympathetic if we get to know and assist them.

It is

also essential to engage in acts of kindness daily, whether assisting a friend, volunteering for a cause that is important to me, or simply finding reasons to be joyful. Even seemingly insignificant actions like this can have a significant impact on the lives of others.

Being kind is another facet of a leader's character. I plan to set off a cascade of generosity by modeling charitable behavior for others around me and encouraging them to emulate my actions.

Lastly, if you want to leave a loving and compassionate legacy, you may develop support networks, be a good role model, perform random acts of kindness, and fight for social justice. Through participation in these events, I hope to foster a culture of compassion and love that will be passed down to future generations.

Because I want to be remembered as a kind and loving person, I am continuously searching for methods to improve the quality of life for other people. I am always seeking new ways to assist others who are less fortunate, whether it is via the donation of money, the performance of volunteer work for charitable organizations, or engagement in activities within my local community.

Gaining knowledge and understanding may assist individuals in being more compassionate toward one another. I am intensely interested in learning about and having conversations about the challenges encountered by people of many ages, worldviews, and financial circumstances. Encouraging individuals to communicate with one another about their experiences may reduce prejudice and increase understanding.

In addition, I have made it a priority to lend a helping hand to those in need. Whether it's via teaching or using my employment to promote compassion and happiness, I want to put my abilities to use so that I may help make the world and the lives of those in it a better place.

My mission in life is to honor and respect everyone I come into contact with and to leave behind a wake of love and thoughtfulness wherever I go. I know how much it can mean to someone, whether they are a friend, a family member, a coworker, or a total stranger when you say something nice to them or do something nice for them.I give the digital tracks I leave behind a lot of attention before I release them. When I'm online, I make it a point to share positive energy with others, discuss topics and activities that lift my spirits, and lend a hand to organizations that share my commitment to altruism and compassion.

In short, if we want to leave a legacy of kindness and compassion to future generations, we need to be proactive in our attempts to serve others, continuously study and grow in consciousness, put our talents and abilities to good use, respect and appreciate everyone, and disseminate positivity in both our offline and online contacts. By conducting my life per these principles, I want to leave a legacy of compassion and thoughtfulness that will last long after I am gone. This ought to inspire us to desire to leave a loving and caring legacy for future generations, which will make the world a better place for those who come after us.

Our society needs to instill a sense of gratitude and appreciation in its members. Thanking individuals for being kind to me is not only the appropriate thing to do but also an effective technique to persuade me to carry out an action. By publicly expressing our gratitude to those who have assisted others, we will encourage additional individuals to act similarly.

Showing compassion toward oneself is essential to making a positive behavioral imprint on others. First, you should give yourself the same level of attention and consideration you provide others. If we are compassionate toward ourselves, we will likely be better able to be compassionate toward others.

I am also conscious of how the decisions I make and what I do influence the world and the people who live in it.I want to teach future generations to care about the natural world for the rest of their lives by helping our planet and its people, being kind to animals, and protecting the natural world.

When young children and teenagers are in my presence, I hope to serve as a positive role model for them. If we take care of future generations' mental and emotional health, teach them empathy, and provide them with the resources they need to make a difference in the world, then love and compassion will be passed on to the generations who come after us.

In my daily routine, I strive to remain aware of opportunities to establish interpersonal connections and assist individuals who present themselves. Engaging in seemingly inconsequential actions, such as offering a smile to an unfamiliar individual, providing service to a distressed friend, or performing spontaneous acts of benevolence, can significantly contribute to the amelioration of our global community.

In the end, leaving behind a kind and compassionate remembrance requires a broad range of skills, including appreciation, self-compassion, environmental awareness, mentoring, and the willingness to realize that even the most minor acts of kindness are vital. These abilities, along with others, are essential. I want to generate a chain reaction of good deeds that will make the world a better place for people now and in the future by following these values in my day-to-day life and making them a part of my daily routine. Let's all make an effort to leave behind a loving and caring legacy that will live on, and while we're doing it, let's also consider how our choices today will impact the generations who follow us.

Chapter 8: Love and Acceptance as a Path Out of Discrimination

In this chapter, I studied how discrimination affects love relationships, and it taught me that discrimination can greatly affect how people treat each other. Kindness and honesty are important to me, so it's important to eliminate discrimination in the community.

I've seen how discrimination can change how two people initially feel about each other. Our unconscious thoughts about race, ethnicity, religion, and other things can affect who we choose as a love partner. This could cause some groups to be left out of dating chances and help people develop bad attitudes.

Discrimination may also be seen in how people interact with one another regularly. Relationships may be shattered, and one's mental health may suffer discrimination between couples may prohibit them from having honest dialogues, limiting their ability to connect with and comprehend one another.

Reflection and a willingness to foster empathy and compassion are essential to combat discrimination within committed partnerships. We may make our encounters with others more inviting and encouraging by becoming aware of and working to overcome our assumptions.

Discrimination has a detrimental influence on communication, chemistry, and other elements of romantic relationships. I am committed to facing and overcoming prejudice to build relationships based on shared values and mutual respect, just as I want to foster love and acceptance. By striving toward a more tolerant and inclusive worldview, we may help eradicate prejudice and support individuals in creating deeper, more rewarding interactions.

While researching prejudice and its consequences on romantic relationships, it is vital to remember that cultural biases might influence how others perceive and handle such connections. Couples from disadvantaged or stigmatized groups may face discrimination and scrutiny from the public.

Prejudice in society can sever bonds. Couples may face additional stress and strain in their relationships as they seek to remove discrimination. They may have to defend their connection in the face of prejudice, social norms, and presumptions.

Internalized prejudice can cause partners to mistrust their values and suffer from low self-esteem. If one or both couples have received negative cultural messages about their identities, it may not be easy to completely accept and express their love for one another.

To overcome prejudice in committed partnerships, two people must be able to talk openly about their feelings and listen to one another without passing judgment. People must work together to eradicate damaging prejudice and preconceptions to establish an inclusive community.

When I examine how discrimination may affect interpersonal relationships, I am reminded of the need to encourage diversity and tolerance in all aspects of society. If we all try to accept and understand one another, we can create a prejudice-free atmosphere in which love may blossom.

Discrimination has a significant detrimental influence on the attractiveness, communication, and overall satisfaction of intimate relationships. Relationships can only be founded on love, acceptance, and respect for one another when discrimination is identified and vigorously opposed. Let us work together to eliminate discrimination and establish a society where everyone may freely love and be loved.

Furthermore, showing solidarity and mutual support in the face of discrimination can deepen romantic relationships. A robust anti-bias coalition can emerge when partners actively safeguard and promote one another's rights and dignity.

Another important step in eliminating discrimination is challenging the cultural norms and attitudes that generate discrimination. With careful preparation and work, we can rewrite history to include more inclusive and diverse love connections.

I'm dedicated to being aware of the biases that may impact my judgments and decisions as I manage my romantic relationships. Love is most powerful when it is free of discrimination. Therefore, I'm committed to learning and dispelling any misconceptions.

It's also important to understand that removing discrimination in intimate relationships is a never-ending process, not a destination. Compassion, curiosity, and a drive to learn and grow are required. Our love becomes deeper as we build mutual understanding and trust.

Reducing discrimination in romantic relationships is a difficult and influential effort. Relationships marked by love, acceptance, and respect for one another may be fostered via open communication, mutual support, challenging traditional knowledge, and a dedication to one's progress. Accepting our personal and social responsibilities to combat discrimination let us work toward a world free discrimination. Doing so may leave a legacy of love that motivates future generations to accept individuals for who they are, regardless of differences.

Everyone must practice tolerance and set aside prejudice to build a more accepting and peaceful atmosphere. Prejudice stems from firmly held views and attitudes that can lead to discrimination and conflict between individuals and groups. We perpetuate injustice and impede strong relationships when we succumb to prejudice and allow it to govern our actions and interactions. Tolerance enables us to accept and cherish one another's differences without bias or judgment. It will enable us to appreciate how others think and understand our differences. We can build a community where people of all identities and origins feel safe and welcome by prioritizing acceptance over exclusion. Tolerance for one another's differences promotes greater understanding, compassion, and collaboration, all of which benefit our community. By setting discrimination aside and embracing tolerance, we eventually make huge progress toward creating a society that thrives on love, acceptance, and mutual respect. As a result, we leave a legacy of compassion and peace for future generations.

The benefits of embracing diversity and mitigating discrimination extend far beyond individual experiences. Embracing tolerance fosters an inclusive atmosphere wherein individuals with diverse backgrounds and viewpoints can coexist harmoniously and efficiently.

Discrimination, conversely, fosters hatred and establishes divisions among individuals. This perpetuates a cycle of discrimination, marginalization, and, in certain instances, bodily injury. The cessation of this recurring pattern and the cultivation of an environment conducive to love and compassion can be achieved through rejecting prejudiced attitudes and adopting a mindset that embraces tolerance.

The cultivation of a climate characterized by tolerance fosters an environment conducive to engaging in open discourse and the exchange of ideas. The potential existence of conflicting perspectives compels individuals to expand their knowledge and acknowledge the multifaceted nature of human experiences.

Moreover, the imperative of valuing diversity is crucial in the effort to address and counteract prejudice within the broader context of society. The systemic origin of this issue can be comprehended by examining and mitigating personal prejudice. Based on the provided information, there is potential advocacy for enacting legislation to safeguard all individuals' fundamental rights.

With the help of tolerance, we may build relationships based on mutual respect and trust. It allows us to form deeper bonds of friendship and community with folks that go beyond our surface similarities.

When I consider the importance of letting go of discrimination and embracing tolerance, I am reminded of the life-changing potential of a global attitude shift. If we choose love and acceptance over hatred and separation, the future may be brighter for everyone, regardless of race, religion, gender, or any other distinguishing feature.

Finally, letting go of prejudice and intolerance is a great force for development. It gives us the tools to build a community that values diversity, actively works against discrimination, and treats one another respectfully and understanding. Let us all strive together to be peacemakers by cultivating a culture of compassion and respect for one another so that future generations might live in peace and prosperity.

Addressing the world's most pressing crises necessitates doing the right thing, recognizing diversity, and putting discrimination aside. In today's globalized world, we must be able to appreciate variety and collaborate across borders if we are to address serious concerns such as climate change, extreme poverty, and lethal violence.

When prejudice veils our judgment, it isn't easy to realize our common humanity. Tolerance allows us to understand that, despite our differences, we all have the same human sentiments and desires for pleasure and contentment. Understanding our shared experiences may foster empathy and unity, allowing us to collaborate for the benefit of all.

A varied and accepting society encourages innovation and creativity. When people from various backgrounds come together, they provide fresh insights and cutting-edge ideas that help to push the boundaries of science, technology, the arts, and culture. Tolerance fosters an atmosphere where innovation may flourish, benefiting society as a whole.

Tolerance is essential because it allows people to overcome barriers and realize their full potential. We can help people reach their full potential by creating an environment where every member of society is appreciated and cared for. Tolerance makes room for greater inclusion and social mobility by eliminating barriers.

Tolerance must also take on the role of fostering peace and settling conflicts. Tolerance may be an effective mediator when discrimination has produced strife in a community. We may begin the healing and forgiving process by empathizing with one another, laying the groundwork for long-term harmony.

I strive to be an open-minded someone who spreads compassion. I understand that daily treating others with respect and compassion is the first step in leaving a legacy of love and acceptance. Treating people fairly and with care will motivate them to do the same for others.

Cultivating tolerance is critical for progress toward a more equal and peaceful world. Collaboration, creativity, and new ideas are encouraged, and societal peace and stability are achieved. By rejecting bigotry and accepting individuals for who they are, we may leave a legacy contributing to a more diverse, peaceful, and successful future for all humanity. Let us all aspire to be more tolerant people who work together to build a more compassionate and understanding society that will leave a loving legacy for our children and grandchildren.

It is inspiring to learn about individuals who have developed a deep affection for one another despite facing seemingly insurmountable challenges. These individuals faced difficulties, such as deeply ingrained cultural norms, language barriers, and physical limitations. Despite various challenges and adversities, they actively pursued a romantic relationship. Individuals overcome challenges by managing their emotions and actively cultivating authentic connections with others. These narratives are pertinent reminders that love can overcome any hindrances and improve the state of the world. This work exemplifies the capacity for individuals, irrespective of their specific circumstances, to attain love and contentment. They persist in serving as exemplars for others by wholeheartedly embracing love in its various manifestations and nurturing a sense of optimism for the endurance of their relationship.

This study provides evidence to support the notion that love has the potential to confront and surpass prevailing societal and cultural stereotypes. Within a specific narrative, one individual's familial and communal networks expressed strong opposition towards the romantic union between this individual and a partner hailing from a distinct cultural background. Despite encountering challenges and facing resistance, the individuals involved demonstrate unwavering dedication to one another and their collective objectives. The deep connection between them serves as a cohesive element, enabling them to surmount challenges and motivating individuals in their proximity to expand their perspectives.

In a fictional case, a person with a disability falls in love with a committed partner who accepts them regardless of their physical or mental limitations. When people with disabilities face problems in a society supporting ableism, their relationships with others get stronger. This makes them more likely to stand up for the rights of people with disabilities. This shows how love can have a big effect because it can cause big changes in the way people think and improve the general well-being of people with different skills.

People can make relationships with other people that aren't limited by where they live, but only in certain situations. Long-distance lovers who overcome language and cultural barriers to get back together are fascinating examples of how love is strong and never-ending. The people's unwavering commitment is a powerful example of how love can cross all borders and bring people together, no matter how far apart they are geographically or how different their cultures are.

The stories above show how prejudice and discrimination can be overcome by using the changing power of love. How these brave people showed affection shows how to get to real love and set an example for others.

The stories above show how important it is to try to find love, no matter how hard it is. People must have certain traits like honesty, resilience, and a belief in the power of love to help them grow and change to pursue loving relationships actively. People need to rethink what they think they know about sexual relationships because love can happen in unexpected and unusual ways. These stories are a gentle reminder to keep an open and receptive mind while appreciating each loving encounter's uniqueness.

In essence, the narratives of individuals who challenged prevailing social conventions and forged romantic relationships in the face of seemingly insurmountable challenges serve as a wellspring of motivation, instilling within us an unwavering belief in the capacity of love to triumph over adversity. These examples serve as a poignant reminder that love can eliminate discrimination and foster cohesion among individuals from various social and cultural backgrounds. Irrespective of the prevailing conditions, these narratives exemplify the inherent ability of individuals to surmount formidable challenges and attain emotional attachment and satisfaction. These narratives function as didactic illustrations, showcasing the importance of embracing the transformative and affirmative voyage of love.

Upon conducting a more thorough analysis, it becomes evident that these accounts of love triumphing over seemingly insurmountable challenges extend beyond romantic entanglements. They also delve into the realms of individual development and self-actualization. The protagonists in these narratives exhibit personal stories and demonstrate signs of

162

maturity as they effectively overcome various challenges and consciously prioritize love over fear.

The experiences of individuals offer valuable insights into the importance of exhibiting compassion, tenacity, and perseverance in the face of challenging circumstances. The study's authors illustrate that love necessitates dedication to undertaking risks and persisting through adversities instead of being a fleeting sentiment.

Due to their disparate religious convictions, a specific couple experiences discrimination. Despite encountering initial resistance from their familial and communal circles, these individuals embarked upon a trajectory characterized by a commitment to acquiring knowledge and a readiness to attain resolutions agreeable to all parties involved. The interrelationship between these individuals catalyzes a shared sense of appreciation and understanding of each other's cultural heritage.

In an alternate narrative, a couple of the same gender endeavors to sustain their affection amidst the challenges posed by societal discrimination and hostility exhibited by their community members. The individuals show bravery in pursuing personal happiness, actively defying societal expectations, and inspiring others to embrace diverse forms of affection.

These narratives illustrate the capacity of love to function as a positive and beneficial force. The unwavering dedication these individuals demonstrate in pursuing their romantic aspirations challenges established norms and biases. Their enduring bond acts as a catalyst for reflection and opposition to the prejudices encountered in our daily existence, thereby promoting the advancement toward a society marked by equity and inclusiveness.

These narratives also exemplify the transcendence of love across geographical boundaries. The entity exhibits a lack of concern towards its surroundings and demonstrates the ability to thrive within social collectives characterized by apparent discord. The romantic relationship between the individuals in question indicates that judging relationships based solely on their outward appearance or public behavior is imprudent.

Individuals are compelled to critically assess their past and question the underlying assumptions and limitations that define their social exchanges as they become engrossed in these captivating narratives. Individuals are often encouraged to adopt a receptive mindset when engaging in romantic relationships, characterized by accepting diversity and acknowledging the profound capacity for personal growth that can arise from human connections.

Narratives that portray the victory of love in the face of hardship serve as compelling exemplifications of the resilient essence of the human spirit and the profound potential of love to bring about beneficial transformations. The individuals mentioned above endorse embracing risks within romantic relationships, actively confronting discriminatory attitudes, and questioning long-standing societal conventions. These narratives provide inspiration for creating a societal framework in which love surpasses limitations and individuals are universally accepted by their beloved counterparts. As individuals traverse their respective journeys, it is imperative to remember the ethical teachings conveyed by these narratives, acknowledging that including affection can yield noteworthy consequences.

Love is an influential sentiment that possesses the capacity to dismantle obstacles and cultivate interpersonal bonds among individuals hailing from varied socio-cultural contexts. It exhibits an intrinsic magnetic characteristic that promotes the convergence of individuals, thereby fostering the cultivation of interpersonal relationships grounded in mutual comprehension and acceptance. The emotion of love enables individuals to surpass their disparities and cultivate a sense of mutual respect for each person's distinct abilities and perspectives. Rather than perceiving our divergences as obstacles to attaining peace and advancement, the notion of love directs us to accept and appreciate them as unique attributes that enhance our identities. The activity promotes the development of compassion, empathy, and cooperation while simultaneously cultivating a sense of comfort and acknowledging the intrinsic worth of individuals.

Love, in its diverse forms, exhibits a significant potential to foster unity among individuals and facilitate the process of emotional and physical healing. The factors mentioned above promote dialogue, reciprocal regard, and a readiness to acquire novel proficiencies from each other. Love is the foundational component that facilitates the integration of appreciation and acceptance within the complex fabric of our ever-changing human existence.

The ability of love to foster interpersonal connections and understanding of individual identities carries societal ramifications that transcend the domain of romantic partnerships. When individuals opt to be guided by the principle of love in their decision-making processes, a series of interconnected events is set in motion, leading to eventual benefits for all involved parties.

When a society stresses the value of love, its members are more likely to be kind and compassionate toward one another. Individuals are motivated by the feeling of love to actively engage in carefully listening to one another's life narratives and experiences, building a heightened understanding of one another, and cementing the interconnection that connects us. The eradication of discriminatory obstacles enhances the capacity to transcend personal prejudices and identify and cherish the unique characteristics inherent in each individual.

Love fosters not only individual acceptance but also a sense of community. If we can learn to accept and appreciate one another's distinct skills, we can create a society in which everyone has the opportunity to flourish. People are free to be themselves and not care what others think when they are in love.

In social justice and activism, love is the primary motivator for the forward movement. We are motivated to take action in the name of social justice when we love one another and regard every individual for who they are in their own right. When individuals are motivated by love to fight against unfair institutions and preserve the rights of underrepresented groups, a more equal and just society will likely be attained.

The power of love to unite individuals extends well beyond romantic or platonic attachments between individuals. In addition, it could encourage people from different parts of the world to work together. When nations and cultures come together with compassion and understanding for one another, it may be possible to address global issues such as climate change, poverty, and international conflicts together.

Love teaches us the worth of comprehending and enjoying one another's unique qualities and the grace that results from locating areas of agreement between individuals. It motivates us to look for solutions that benefit both parties. When love can carry a relationship through challenging times, the union will eventually grow stronger and more long-lasting.

Last but not least, love is essential in bringing people together and embracing their individuality. Our romantic and platonic partnerships, as well as our engagement in our communities, are all affected. The power of love may lead to a more compassionate and peaceful society due to its ability to remove barriers, foster empathy, and inspire positive change. We can leave a lasting mark of respect and collaboration for future generations by keeping an open mind toward love and its transformative power.

It will be easier to appreciate love's potential to heal and transform individuals and communities as we understand pets' changing role in bringing people together and accepting each person's unique qualities to the group. Because love has enormous potential to heal wounds and connect people who have been divided, adversity often presents a chance for personal development and peacemaking.

Love encourages us to approach individuals with compassion and understanding, even when we have differences of opinion with them. It teaches us to set aside our preconceived notions and consider the perspectives and ideas of the people we encounter. People are more willing to forgive one another and move on from negative experiences when they are driven by love rather than revenge or resentment.

Love compels us to recognize and cherish the uniqueness of our perspectives and experiences and to do so with appreciation. We can gain a broader perspective on the world when we open our minds to others whose backgrounds, thoughts, and views differ. Love piques our attention, enabling us to gain fresh insights about one another and forge deeper connections with our fellow people.

In a broken and fractured society, love has the power to unite individuals even though they are different from one another. It compels us to speak with one another and search for areas of common ground. Love makes us set aside our disagreements and cooperate for the sake of the larger good because it teaches us that our satisfaction is directly proportional to the joy experienced by others around us.

By fostering a loving attitude among our neighbors, we may work toward creating neighborhoods in which everyone can feel comfortable being themselves without fear of repercussions. When there is love in the room, everyone is more at ease expressing themselves freely and knowing their thoughts and ideas will be treated seriously. It helps foster the growth of welcoming communities where individuals of all abilities are encouraged to flourish and share their unique gifts.

The influence of love on society's rules and values extends well beyond personal relationships. Cultures that emphasize compassion and tolerance are more likely to uphold democratic principles and the rule of law throughout their history. People are motivated to take action to better the resources and opportunities available to everyone when they are motivated by love.

Last but not least, love possesses an inexplicable and transformational force that may bring people together and teach them to accept one another's individuality. It has an unlimited capacity to bring about reconciliation, unity, and constructive transformation. When we make love the guiding principle in our interpersonal and social connections, we leave a legacy of compassion, acceptance, and peace in our communities and the world. Let us spread the love so that the next generation will be inspired to build relationships that respect differences, emphasize similarities, and collaborate to improve the world.

The capacity to love can bring about a shift on a global scale as well as the development of a more compassionate and interconnected society. This impact is not limited to a particular relationship or culture. When love motivates our deeds and choices, our relationship with the land and the people there shifts.

Regarding pressing issues affecting the world, such as poverty, climate change, and natural catastrophes, love motivates us to take greater responsibility and more vigorous action. Because we care about the environment and want to ensure that it will be here for future generations, we engage in ecologically friendly activities. Because we care about people, we have a responsibility to tackle the underlying problems that lead to poverty and inequality, and we should work toward creating a more fair society so that everyone has access to the resources they require to be successful.

Love also plays a significant role in shaping the methods employed to address conflicts and establish peace. In instances of violent situations, the emotion of love motivates individuals to adopt the victim's perspective rather than that of the perpetrator, thereby prompting the search for nonviolent resolutions. Love is the singular force that can unite individuals, dismantle obstacles impeding communication and comprehension, and establish the fundamental groundwork for enduring tranquility and conciliation.

Moreover, love engenders a sense of interconnectedness and unity with the broader global community. By demonstrating acts of kindness and compassion towards individuals, irrespective of their race, religion, gender, sexual orientation, or socioeconomic status, we actively break down the societal divisions that separate us. The dynamic nature of love's influence is a pertinent reminder that a fundamental interconnectedness exists among individuals, binding us together as members of a shared human lineage.

As our understanding of the profound capacity of love to engender a society characterized by greater equity and harmony deepens, we must embrace our responsibility as catalysts for constructive transformation. To effectively pursue the goals of social justice and the advancement of marginalized communities, individuals must be driven by a sense of love and compassion. The experience fosters self-confidence within individuals, empowering them to actively support fairness and engage in efforts to rectify systemic disparities.

Love can transform the commercial and political environment by persuading leaders to prioritize their constituency and the planet's requirements over opportunities to increase their financial gain. When compassion is at the forefront of policies, we see inclusive economic growth and the protection of those at the bottom of the socioeconomic ladder.

In the end, love is a powerful emotion that has a wide-reaching and important impact on the world. It can start a revolution on a worldwide scale and bring about the day when humans and the environment may coexist harmoniously in all parts of the world. As we carry on the tradition of love, we know that every individual's actions, regardless of how insignificant they may seem, contribute to a broader global change toward more compassion and connectivity. Let us not stop sowing the seeds of love wherever we go because we know it will lead to a better and more equitable tomorrow for everyone.

Chapter 9: The Healer: Love and Forgiveness

Forgiveness may be a powerful approach to healing broken relationships with others. By deciding to forgive, we may release any pent-up bitterness or hostility. If resentments are held in the heart, the wounds will not heal. Forgiveness, as a tool for self-empowerment and emotional emancipation, is not the same as admitting guilt or excusing harmful behavior.

As we forgive, we allow ourselves to feel pity and gain perspective. This perspective shift may help one feel more sympathy and empathy for the individual who caused the misery. This allows for more open conversation and the prospect of reestablishing trusting relationships.

Furthermore, forgiveness has the potential to function as a catalyst for improvement and advancement. We create a place in our brains and hearts for brighter feelings like love and compassion when we release suppressed anger. This mental and emotional development may benefit everyone involved, opening the door to improved dialogue and mutual acceptance.

It may be extremely therapeutic and transformational, even if it is tough to forgive someone when relationships have been harmed. Putting the past behind you and working with others to build a better future takes courage, vulnerability, and a genuine willingness to let go of the past. When we choose to forgive, we give ourselves and the other person the gift of experiencing the changing power of love.

The ability to forgive is a sign of personal development and mental and emotional maturity. Accepting our grief and choosing the road of healing over repeating the same detrimental patterns of anger and bitterness needs courage and awareness. We express our gratitude for the relationship and our resolve to repair it by forgiving.

A shared capacity for forgiveness might serve as a foundation for healing damaged ties. By forgiving, we admit our flaws and the possibility that others, like us, may make mistakes. This understanding makes peace possible by making people more empathetic and self-aware.

Also, forgiving someone might make them think about what they did and take responsibility for it. If we forgive those who have hurt us, they may feel like they have to do the same. This will strengthen your friendship and make you more willing to work on it.

It's critical to remember that forgiving someone else isn't always easy. Dealing with emotions, especially those that are truly unpleasant, requires work and time. Allow yourself as much time as you need to emotionally recuperate before forgiving. Forgiving someone too quickly may backfire and prevent you from experiencing true healing.

After forgiveness, a relationship may not always be completely restored, especially if the previous encounter was poisonous or violent. In many cases, forgiveness becomes a form of emotional liberation that allows the forgiver to move on from the past and continue with their life.

Finally, it is critical to remember that forgiveness has the incredible capacity to restore damaged interpersonal ties. It frees us from the burden of our negative emotions, opens a place for understanding and compassion among others, and paves the road for personal serenity and progress. By choosing to forgive, we exhibit our confidence in the power of love and respect for our relationships with others. Even though ignoring someone does not always make things right between them, it may still help you grow and heal so that you may approach life and your relationships with greater understanding and compassion.

Forgiveness is a freeing act that benefits both the forgiver and the forgiving. We give the past authority over our present and future when we hang onto resentment and refuse to forgive. It keeps us in a negative loop, stopping us from truly enjoying love, serenity, and enjoyment.

When we forgive others, we release ourselves from the psychological prison of bitterness and anger. We may sigh with relief now that the weight has been lifted off our shoulders. This creates an atmosphere where good feelings such as love, compassion, and understanding flourish.

Forgiving someone can also aid in one's growth and emotional rehabilitation. To do so, we must accept both our flaws and the pain we have endured. This teaches us more about ourselves and how our emotions function. If we possessed this level of insight, we could change our behavior and make better decisions in our interpersonal relationships.

Forgiving wrongdoing contributes to the development of a more compassionate and inviting heart. When we forgive others, we make a place for new relationships and chances to enter our lives. It allows us to interact with people on a deeper, more meaningful level via mutual understanding and trust.

Forgiveness may enhance our emotional and physical health and repair damaged relationships. According to research, carrying anger and resentment may harm one's mental and physical health. On the other hand, forgiving someone has been shown to influence one's physical and psychological health positively.

Furthermore, forgiving someone is an ongoing process rather than a one-time event. Even after we have forgiven someone, the pain of the crime may reemerge on occasion. It is critical at this point to revisit your decision to forgive and reaffirm your commitment to the healing process.

In short, forgiveness is a potent weapon that can alter our life path and relationships with others. It provides us the confidence to leave the past behind us and focus on our future progress and wellness. When we choose to forgive, we let go of negative emotions and make room in our hearts for positive ones. Although it is a never-ending process that needs bravery, the rewards of pleasure, connection, and health make it worthwhile.

Love has a long way to go, even after forgiving someone. While forgiveness may be a powerful motivator for healing and reconciliation, the grief and suffering that has already occurred remain. Reestablishing trust after forgiveness takes a lot of effort on both sides.

It is a difficult effort to rebuild trust. After trust has been shattered, it may take time to rebuild. You may be hesitant to trust someone again if they have already harmed you, fearing that they would do it again. Before you regain people's trust, you must be trustworthy, talk honestly, and demonstrate a shift in conduct.

Another obstacle is overcoming the psychological and emotional scars of the past. Emotional scars may persist even after seeking and receiving forgiveness. Residual feelings of fury, grief, or insecurity may limit the offended party's capacity to commit to the relationship completely. To build a better emotional foundation, both partners must be willing to accept and confront these emotions.

Peer, familial, and social pressures and judgments may also occur. Others will disagree with your decision to forgive, and others may doubt that you two can ever be friends again. Dealing with opposing points of view may make the process of repairing and building a relationship even more difficult.

Fear of being injured again can sometimes thwart love after forgiveness. Someone who has harmed you may be afraid to be emotionally open for fear of causing you hurt again. However, the sufferer may retreat to avoid more suffering.

There may be difficulties, but there will be huge rewards in love after forgiving. As a result, the bond between two people who have shared adversity may strengthen. It has the potential to forge a friendship based on persistence, knowledge, and a common desire to progress.

Following forgiveness of misbehavior, the connection must be rebuilt and maintained. Both sides must be patient, sensitive, and willing to put in the effort to achieve this. Respect each other's emotional needs and always keep communication channels open. Love after forgiveness can bloom into a magnificent and transforming journey of healing and growth if given enough time, comprehension, and honest effort.

Another impediment is the likelihood of future violations. The forgiven party may be apprehensive that the perpetrator will continue to harm others. When you're always on edge due to fear, relaxing your guard and putting your faith in your spouse is tough. For the one who inflicted the harm, constantly having to demonstrate one's changed intentions can be stressful and strain the relationship.

Furthermore, they may both struggle to let go of the past. Although it is an important first step in healing, forgiving someone does not diminish the weight of their previous actions or the memories associated with them. Repairing the relationship may be hindered by continuously addressing or dwelling on unpleasant occurrences. To make progress, we must accept the present and collaborate to create a positive future.

Communication problems may impede couples from having good relationships after they have forgiven each other. Expressing desires, worries, and feelings freely and honestly is critical. It may be difficult for the afflicted individual to articulate their vulnerabilities and requirements for fear of causing greater grief. The person who wounded you may be experiencing grief or defensiveness, making it difficult for them to listen closely and respond compassionately.

Furthermore, forgiveness does not always result in a restored relationship. Despite your best efforts and repeated attempts at mending, the association is unlikely to return to its former liveliness. Both persons will likely have undergone substantial changes due to their loss, and their objectives, aspirations, and interests are no longer in sync. In such a circumstance, the emotional difficulty of realizing that the relationship may no longer be salvageable intensifies.

Despite the aforementioned obstacles, a substantial number of individuals believe that the experience of love following forgiveness results in positive outcomes. This opportunity allows individuals to broaden their perspectives and advance their personal development. As a result, individuals may develop qualities of compassion and understanding. Although it may not be possible to fully restore the relationship to its former state, cultivating mutual respect and experience can facilitate its transformation into a more substantial bond.

In other words, the path toward experiencing love following an act of forgiveness is lengthy and difficult. Both partners must possess emotional security, receptivity, and commitment for this to succeed. The imperatives of restoring trust, facilitating the healing of emotional wounds, managing external expectations, mitigating anxieties, and removing barriers to effective communication are just some of the critical issues that require attention. Nonetheless, the experience of love following the act of forgiveness has the potential to cultivate improved communication, greater tolerance, and a sincere desire for self-improvement. These positive outcomes have the potential to promote healing and personal growth for both parties involved.

The concept of forgiveness is universal, transcending geographical and cultural boundaries, and can transform the lives of people from diverse origins. An individual who suffered significant loss due to a catastrophic event caused by another person's negligence serves as an example. The individuals had difficulty overcoming their initial feelings of wrath and grief. Initially hindered by feelings of resentment and anger, the individuals were ultimately liberated by the act of forgiveness. Despite its inability to reverse historical events, the act of repentance demonstrated by the individuals, as mentioned earlier, delivered them from feelings of hatred and empowered them to move forward.

The second incredible tale also involves a close friendship that ultimately leads to hurt and betrayal. The trust had been broken so badly that it appeared difficult to repair, and the damage created by a misunderstanding inside the family felt insurmountable. They were hesitant to forgive at first but eventually came to terms with the fact that harboring resentment would only compound their suffering. The people went through a process of liberation and renewal by forgiving both themselves and those who had wronged them. People's connections with others in their social circles improved as a result of their willingness to forgive and make amends with one another.

There is also a tale of someone harboring deep resentment towards a distant relative from whom they had been estranged for quite some time. It was seen that their mental and physical health suffered greatly as a result of their emotional catastrophes. The individuals could acknowledge their suffering and find relief by adopting a new way of life that prioritizes compassion. When individuals are able to accept one another, it creates an environment where they may develop emotionally and personally. They were able to reconnect with their loved ones and experience deeper levels of respect and appreciation for one another after practicing forgiveness.

The following narratives illustrate the profound effects of mercy and forgiveness on a person's life. When you forgive someone, you begin the healing process, you can go on with your life, and you have a fresh outlook on things. When people aren't hostile toward one another, they're better equipped to work together to solve difficulties. These accounts are a moving testimony to the transformative potential of forgiveness in the lives of those who are willing to receive it.

The protagonist must make a difficult ethical decision when they discover a close friend has lied. People considered cutting off communication or taking vengeance but ultimately decided to forgive. After making amends and asking for forgiveness, the rift was healed, and a fresh perspective was granted. People's initial reluctance to forgive and put an end to their battles is overcome when they make the deliberate decision to do so. The people's capacity to forgive one another strengthened their connections and brought them more happiness and contentment.

During that moment, someone admitted that they were harboring resentment and hatred toward a former coworker who had severely damaged their reputation in the workplace. The individual's elevated emotional state impedes their ability to make sound decisions, stunting their career and personal development. However, as society improved its capacity for forgiveness, individuals realized that holding grudges hindered their stories. Those who were able to forgive their oppressors ultimately flourished as persons and achieved wonderful things.

The protagonist in the novel suffers physically and emotionally because of their inability to let go of the consequences of their actions. People felt dreadful because persistent feelings of guilt and shame damaged their sense of self-worth. As a result, I suffered a great deal emotionally. Conversely, self-forgiveness aided individuals in acknowledging their shortcomings and realizing their inherent worth. Self-forgiveness practitioners reported profound shifts in their sense of self-worth. Because of this, they were better able to accept and love one another.

These examples demonstrate that forgiveness is about more than merely mending fences. It also entails acknowledging and fixing one's own shortcomings. Individuals can grow from their experiences, become more resilient and flexible, and ultimately live a life that provides them fulfillment. These narratives illustrate the positive effects of forgiving oneself and others. They also provide solace and inspiration to those in need of those things.

One of the most effective means of cultivating empathy and compassion is forgiving oneself for past transgressions. Both the development and healing of the heart rely on this mechanism. Compassion for oneself and others can be stunted by feelings of regret, guilt, and self-blame stemming from previous mistakes or failures. Self-forgiveness frees individuals to treat themselves with compassion and acceptance rather than harsh judgment. When we practice forgiveness toward ourselves, we remove obstacles to true self-acceptance and love. Understanding our inherent humanity and accepting that making errors is a normal aspect of being human is facilitated by cultivating compassion, which involves self-compassion and kindness for others. When you practice self-compassion, it becomes easier to be loving and kind to others in social circumstances. After you've learned to forgive yourself, it's easier to forgive other people. This way of practicing self-compassion can lead to more self-love and respect and more love and care for other people.

Self-love and self-compassion can only grow once you learn to forgive yourself. We create an environment of self-criticism and self-doubt when we don't forgive ourselves for past mistakes or what we think are our flaws and instead focus on these things. If we do this kind of tough self-criticism all the time, it could hurt our efforts to love and care for ourselves and others.

The first step toward forgiving yourself is to admit that you are weak and likely to do wrong. The idea here is that a person's natural value shouldn't be taken away just because they made a mistake. Instead, mistakes are a part of being human and shouldn't be taken away from them. To find inner peace and happiness, you have to forgive yourself and move on.

Self-forgiveness is the first step on the road to self-acceptance and self-love. People can heal from their mental hurts by being more patient and kind to themselves. This process makes us feel better about ourselves, which shows how we treat others. Having a deeper love for oneself makes it easier to set limits and put one's wants first. This makes it possible to have better relationships with other people.

Being able to accept yourself is an important part of being emotionally strong. It helps people get over failures and see problems as possible growth chances. Being able to keep going through hard times builds character and makes us more compassionate toward ourselves and others.

Self-forgiveness is a must if you want to love other people. Most of the time, our guilt and anger make it hard for us to love and accept people without conditions. Getting better at caring for ourselves and forgiving ourselves can help us have better relationships with others.

Self-forgiveness is so important to love that it can't be said enough. Self-compassion is a practice that can help people stop being hard on themselves and learn to accept and love themselves despite their flaws. Self-forgiveness helps us love ourselves and stay strong, improving our relationships with others. The more we work on building our ability to love, the better our relationships with other people are and the more fulfilled we feel in life.

Forgiving yourself can be a strong way to grow and build better relationships with others. When we accept ourselves, we can see the good in ourselves and others more clearly. Understanding the problems and limits of people in our local area helps us connect with them in a better, more caring way.

When communicating with others, self-forgiveness exposes our level of honesty. Once we have internalized self-love and forgiveness, we can be candid with others and let them come to know the true us. Allowing people to see us as we are, without any masks or barriers, leads to a greater sense of closeness and connection. When we treat ourselves with compassion and humility, we attract like-minded people because of tolerance and openness.

Self-forgiveness also keeps one from repeating bad habits. When we do not forgive ourselves, we continue to injure ourselves and others, maintaining the vicious cycle. However, self-forgiveness breaks the pattern and allows for growth and development. We can make clearer, more liberated decisions in our relationships now that we have more mental and emotional space to consider things.

Self-forgiveness gives us the ability to establish realistic limits in our interpersonal connections. When we are at peace with ourselves, we can better identify when others are crossing our boundaries and take the appropriate actions to safeguard our emotional well-being. It develops an atmosphere of understanding and peace by allowing us to forgive people for their errors and whatever pain they have unwittingly caused us.

Aside from interpersonal relationships, self-forgiveness is critical to health and happiness. Self-forgiveness has been related to decreased levels of stress, anxiety, and depression, according to a study. This emotional toughness pervades their connections with others, making it easier to resolve disagreements and encouraging open communication and mutual support.

Finally, self-forgiveness is an important component of both internal and outward love. When we practice being kind and forgiving to ourselves, we make room for development and emotional recovery. It allows us to form genuine connections with other people based on esteem, honesty, and acceptance. When we free ourselves from self-criticism and judgment, we are better equipped to develop love, compassion, and empathy in our relationships, resulting in stronger and more rewarding connections with the people we care about.

Relationships flourish and develop when both partners can forgive one another and move on from past wrongs. Couples may connect freely and emotionally open up to one another by forgiving one another, which is essential for creating trust and a solid bond. Recognizing and letting go of earlier grudges is a key step in emotional healing for the offended individual and the partnership. Children learn to understand one another and to be nice even when things are difficult.

It is critical to forgive and move past marital problems and misunderstandings. Tolerant partners are more prone to explore alternatives to blame or revenge to resolve conflicts. This method promotes a collaborative environment where issues may be investigated and resolved. If both people feel forgiven and accepted, they are likelier to speak up about their feelings and form a stronger emotional link.

Emotional healing, on the other hand, assists couples in addressing any unresolved issues or painful past events that may influence their relationship. Teams that emphasize their mental health increase their ability to help one another through stressful times. Couples that have gone through emotional recovery are better equipped to deal with life's challenges as a team.

With the help of forgiveness and emotional healing, couples may transcend destructive relationship patterns. Unresolved issues from the past may lead to future conflicts and defensive behaviors. This vicious cycle may be broken if partners can work through their feelings and forgive each other.

As a result, the health of any intimate connection is dependent on forgiveness and emotional healing. They strengthen relationships by encouraging the development of trust, empathy, and a willingness to be honest and vulnerable with one another. Couples may progressively improve their relationship by learning to forgive one another and stressing emotional healing whenever there is a quarrel.

Apologizing and making amends for hurt feelings help one's relational, emotional intelligence. When couples have healed their wounds and learned to forgive one another, they can better understand their emotional signs and needs. Because they are more in touch with their emotions, they can better sympathize with and learn from one another's experiences.

Forgiveness and emotional healing may promote a more pleasant dynamic environment in the partnership. Forgiven couples report higher levels of relationship fulfillment and happiness. By letting go of their anger and resentment, people can feel more good emotions such as love, joy, and gratitude. When two people in a relationship feel comfortable and protected, their emotional ties strengthen.

In terms of growth and development, forgiveness and emotional healing assist both people in a relationship. When people tackle their fears and anxieties, they may begin to heal and grow as people. The partnership benefits as a result of each partner's personal development and increased self-awareness, emotional maturity, and desire to support the other's development.

Furthermore, emotional healing and forgiveness can be used to reduce stress. Couples who have mastered forgiving one another and letting go of past grudges are better prepared to face challenges. Rather than allowing arguments to linger and degrade the relationship, they might address difficulties with empathy and a desire to collaborate to discover solutions.

Finally, a partnership may develop a culture of understanding and compassion through forgiving and emotionally repairing past wrongs. Couples that understand each other's ability for forgiveness and healing share a shared dedication to the happiness and personal progress of the other. When both partners are active in each other's emotional well-being, a strong sense of emotional closeness and connectivity occurs, boosting the quality of the relationship.

Finally, forgiveness and emotional healing are the foundations of a good love connection. They foster emotional intelligence, provide a supportive environment, and stimulate personal growth. Forgiveness and emotional healing assist partners in creating a deep dynamic link by creating a climate of understanding and compassion. With the help of forgiveness and emotional healing, couples may develop a strong bond that can withstand life's inevitable storms.

Forgiving and apologizing for hurt feelings has the additional benefit of increasing emotional closeness and connection between spouses. People feel emotionally connected to one another when they can disclose their most private thoughts and feelings to another without fear of rejection or condemnation. Couples who can forgive and be forgiven might feel confident enough to be real with one another. They are more emotionally attached, strengthening their relationship and fostering a sense of belonging.

Couples' relationships benefit from emotional healing brought about by forgiveness. Poor communication can lead to misunderstandings and confrontations due to unresolved wounds and emotions from the past. When couples focus on forgiving and mending their emotional scars, they acquire greater communication skills such as active listening, empathy, and assertiveness. They develop empathy for one another, allowing them to show love and support for one another and resolve disputes in a healthier and more fruitful manner.

Partners may also rewrite their relationship's past by performing acts of forgiveness and emotional healing. As a result of previous fights and traumas, a couple may act and think destructively. If partners are willing to forgive and heal, they can let go of these destructive stories and develop a new one based on love, growth, and mutual understanding. When couples alter their viewpoint in this way, they can better focus on the countless benefits of their partnership and construct a shared future based on their shared values.

While conquering challenges, forgiveness and emotional healing provide strength. Every marriage goes through difficult moments, yet forgiveness allows them to survive with compassion and understanding. After emotional healing, they can better regulate their emotions, and disagreements between them are less likely to destroy their relationship. As a result, partnerships that have been tested may emerge stronger and more committed than before.

Finally, the repercussions of emotional healing and forgiveness may benefit a relationship. Because of the relationship-transforming benefits of forgiveness, it may be applied outside of romantic relationships. They learn to be more compassionate and forgiving via their encounters with others, which spreads kindness across their communities.

Finally, emotional healing and forgiveness can help build love relationships in several ways. They promote communication, emotionally bring partners closer together, and enrich the story of their relationship. Couples who have forgiven each other are more resilient and approach conflict with more compassion and understanding. When a team works on emotional forgiveness and healing inside their union, it affects other aspects of their lives. Love and compassion may flourish in a partnership when hurtful feelings are forgiven and healed.

Chapter 10:Unconditional love is loving despite difficulties.

This crucial section examines how the uncommon concept of unadulterated love can be applied to intimate relationships. Pure love entails a promise to be there for your companion in both happy and bad times. It denotes a connection that endures even as one's beliefs evolve.

When establishing a strong connection between two individuals, it is crucial to emphasize the significance of pure affection. It is an affection that can endure life's disasters and help them overcome problems together. Couples who vow to spend their lives together can strengthen their bond and prepare for the inevitable disasters.

The foundation of unconditional love is accepting a companion despite or due to their faults. It instructs readers to disregard the apparent symptoms of shallowness and instead concentrate on what makes each unique. Anyone can feel at home and accepted for who they are because unadulterated love from a companion provides an unrivaled sense of safety and acceptance.

Additionally, sacrifice and acceptance are characteristics of this form of affection. It entails placing one's needs and objectives on hold to fulfill one's partner's needs and desires. In an unconditionally loving relationship, each partner actively endeavors to understand the other's perspective without rendering judgment.

Moreover, unconditional love fosters the growth and restoration of a couple's relationship. Unconditional affection between spouses enables them to withstand adversity together. They provide constant support and the fortitude to endure difficult times, which fosters personal development and community building. People in a secure and supportive environment can recover and grow closer to one another.

Unconditional affection necessitates a willingness to forgive. Genuine forgiveness and the desire to move on without holding grievances are made possible by unconditional love, which is essential in a relationship because partners are doomed to make mistakes and accidentally injure one another. It is a suggestion to ignore the past and focus on the present and the future.

Due to its compassionate nature, unconditional love fosters emotional connection and trust between lovers. When two individuals unconditionally adore one another, they can be themselves without fear of rejection. The degree of intimacy that results from such an emotional connection can be a positive force in any relationship.

Partners can choose to emphasize or embrace unconditional affection. Working towards the pleasure and well-being of the companion requires effort, self-awareness, and genuine dedication. Throughout the ups and downs of a relationship, unconditional love acts as a compass, fostering personal development and assisting both partners in attaining their maximum potential.

A relationship's health and longevity ultimately rely on a strong, long-lasting emotional connection. Partners who show such constant love can better handle life's problems because they know their partner will always be there for them. Growing pure love is important for a relationship to last, for emotions to grow, and for boundless care to show.

This important part of the study examines the new idea of pure love and how it deeply affects close relationships. Unconditional love can be considered a promise to always be loyal, no matter what problems or changes arise in a connection. It goes beyond passing feelings to include love that stays the same no matter what.

It's important to stress how important pure love is to build a strong link between two people. This love can stand up to the ups and downs of life and the problems they will have to face together. Couples who believe in love that doesn't change can build a strong base to help them overcome the bumps and changes they will encounter on their journey together.

The most important part of pure love is accepting your partner despite their flaws. This trend pushes people to look beyond superficial signs and see the worth and uniqueness of each person for who they are. A partner's unconditional love creates a deep sense of safety and acceptance. This makes everyone feel like they fit in and confirms who they are.

This kind of love is also defined by effort and understanding. It means putting the needs and wants of the other person ahead of your own goals and needs. In a relationship based on pure love, both people try to see things from the other person's point of view without judging.

Moreover, unconditional love fosters the growth and restoration of a couple's relationship. Unconditional affection between spouses enables them to withstand adversity together. They provide constant support and the fortitude to endure difficult times, which fosters personal development and community building. People in a secure and supportive environment can recover and grow closer to one another.

Unconditional affection necessitates a willingness to forgive. Genuine forgiveness and the desire to move on without holding grievances are made possible by unconditional love, which is essential in a relationship because partners are doomed to make mistakes and accidentally injure one another. It is a suggestion to ignore the past and focus on the present and the future.

Due to its compassionate nature, unconditional love fosters emotional connection and trust between lovers. When two individuals unconditionally adore one another, they can be themselves without fear of rejection. The degree of intimacy that results from such an emotional connection can be a positive force in any relationship.

Partners can choose to emphasize or embrace unconditional affection. Working towards the pleasure and well-being of the companion requires effort, self-awareness, and genuine dedication. Throughout the ups and downs of a relationship, unconditional love acts as a compass, fostering personal development and assisting both partners in attaining their maximum potential.

Lastly, the health and longevity of any relationship depend on a firm foundation of unwavering affection. Partners who demonstrate this kind of unconditional affection are better able to confront life's challenges because they know they have the support of their partner. It is essential to emphasize unconditional love for a relationship to endure, develop in terms of emotional connection, and produce boundless affection.

The resilience and tenacity of love in the face of adversity exemplify the profundity and potential of human connection. If two people are genuinely in love, they can surmount any difficulty in their relationship. Hardship includes external expectations, financial problems, health issues, and interpersonal conflicts. However, the unbreakable love between the two people gives them the will and fortitude to overcome adversity.

When difficulties arise in a relationship, affection enables both parties to face them head-on with mutual support. It strengthens your resolve to overcome long-term rather than short-term obstacles. When two people truly adore one another, they can easily set aside their differences and collaborate to find a solution that works for both.

Love requires being forthright and honest in times of difficulty. Partners can discuss their challenges openly and honestly without fear of being condemned. Couples who can communicate publicly and legally become emotionally closer and are better equipped to assist one another in difficult circumstances.

What lends love its tenacity is its propensity for growth and change. When confronted with adversity, a couple may need to modify their goals, desires, or plans. Even when the future appears bleak, they may remain adaptable and enthusiastic to work due to their unending affection for one another.

Additionally, love inspires perseverance and trust. When positive memories are recalled, and future goals and aspirations are discussed, couples' relationships improve. Together, they confront obstacles, but their affection for one another gives them the strength to persevere.

Love requires extending and receiving grace and forgiveness when things go awry. Each companion knows that they can continually progress and that errors are inevitable. Love compels partners to prioritize the present over the past, placing the relationship above trivial concerns.

Love is stronger when it is willing to persevere in adversity rather than giving up at the first hint of trouble. Every relationship will endure challenges, but a committed couple can confront them full-on because they know their love is well worth it.

A couple's dedication to one another exemplifies a deep love that survives through adversity. It's a great example of how love can bloom in trouble. When a partner's love remains unwavering in the face of adversity, it strengthens their bond and reinforces their conviction that they can overcome any barrier together.

Love's courage and tenacity in difficult circumstances are significant since they are individual and changeable. Adversity serves as a litmus test for real love and makes it stronger and more durable. When two individuals share their tales, it demonstrates how much they care for each other, even when things are difficult. This love is like a beacon, pointing the way forward and showing that human ties are always powerful. Even when there are issues, love may triumph if the two people are dedicated to each other and desire to grow as individuals and as a couple.

When examined, love's continual drive and long-lasting character may result in significant changes in personal growth and ties with others. When people learn to rely on one another during difficult circumstances, they frequently discover abilities they did not realize they possessed. As their love for each other deepens, they acquire the fortitude to overcome their weaknesses and confront the difficulties in their outside worlds.

When two individuals attempt to discover love and solve issues together, their connection grows stronger. Couples may strengthen their bond and trust by doing activities together. They can also learn more about one another's characteristics and ideals. As the two persons encounter and handle numerous obstacles, their relationship grows stronger, demonstrating their dedication to one another.

Long-term love can also cause you to reflect on yourself and evolve. When partners collaborate to tackle difficult challenges, they might learn about their strengths, weaknesses, and opportunities for development. People may enhance their emotional intelligence and self-control by noticing and assessing their emotions.

We may also learn much about how crucial it is to collaborate from our challenges. People unite to solve challenges and demonstrate a willingness to give up items for the greater good. This indicates that they work better together than they do alone. Both of them consider the other to be their best friend, which strengthens their bond.

Also, how they show love in hard times can serve as an example for those around them. The fact that a love relationship can stay together even when things are hard shows how important empathy is and how it can change how people live their lives. The person's actions encourage others to use love as a guiding principle in their relationships, even when things get tough.

Though love is strong, it is important to remember that it cannot fix all problems. Despite everyone's best efforts and steadfast devotion, certain difficulties are insurmountable. The strength of love reveals itself in these situations through the ability to accept reality while being unwaveringly supportive of one another.

Love's perseverance and resilience in the face of adversity show the core of the human soul. It is a shining example of honesty, kindness, and grit. True love transcends all obstacles, indicating that even in the most terrible situations, there is always hope and light in the bonds we establish with the people we care about.

Finally, love's ability to endure hardship is critical to evolving and staying. When a couple overcomes difficulties and utilizes love as guidance, they grow as individuals and a partnership. Their bond has become more durable in adversity due to their shared experiences, personal growth, and steadfast dedication. The power of love has far-reaching impacts, inspiring others around us and reminding us of the need for true human connection.

Throughout my life, I have seen many wonderful real-world couples that supported one another through difficult times and prevailed. After losing their job, one team I know faced financial difficulties, but they overcame it together. They established a financial security strategy, looked for alternative career prospects, and gave each other constant emotional support. Their tenacity and mutual spiritual support carried them through the difficult period and into financial security.

Another couple I know overcame a difficult illness. When one of them became ill, the other stepped up to be their primary carer and rock. They coped with a lot, including doctor appointments, tough treatment decisions, and the emotional burden of dealing with a loved one's sickness. The force of their love and determination tremendously benefited them in their quest for health and wholeness.

I also saw a couple mourning the death of a child. Despite the tragedy they had all suffered, they sought solace in one another. They went through the grieving process together, seeking counselors and supporting one another. They became closer over time and found consolation in one another's company, which eventually helped them heal from the disaster.

These couples are examples of love, teamwork, and persistence. They were closer to one another and were better equipped to assist one another when they faced difficulties together. These true stories demonstrate how love can alter a person and how crucial it is to have a companion by your side while you confront life's challenges.

I know a couple that went through infertility treatment for several years. They faced various challenges on their path to becoming parents. They clung to one other and tried to endure the emotional ups and downs together. They went through infertility counseling together, openly sharing their feelings and depending on one another for support. They persisted because of their great bond and desire to start a family, and they finally adopted a kid. The obstacles they overcame enhanced their relationship, and they now appreciate each other and their parenting gift more than ever.

I've witnessed another couple sustain a long-distance relationship despite opposing work schedules. Despite being separated by thousands of miles, they maintained regular contact, traveled frequently together, and made the most of their time together. They overcame the difficulties of separation because they had a strong love for one another and a clear vision for their future together. They could rejoin permanently after a period of separation that strengthened them both and made them more appreciative of their time together since their love for one another was indestructible.

One remarkable pair I know rejected societal and cultural pressures to pursue a romantic connection. Their family originally disapproved of their union since they hailed from different social backgrounds. They consciously decided to stay together because of their undying love. They were honest and upfront with their family members, making a delicate attempt to break cultural boundaries and express their love. Their family finally showed gratitude for their love and the joy they brought into each other's lives. They were able to marry despite family and friends' misgivings because of their undying love for one another.

These real-life couples show how support, love, and determination can bring us through difficult times. They had to deal with money, disease, cultural shame, and physical and emotional separation from loved ones. On the other hand, their undying love for one another inspired them to conquer their hurdles and, consequently, grow closer. Their personal experiences encourage us to believe in the power of love and the perseverance of a dedicated connection.

The vital roles that empathy and compassion played along the way on this trip of enormous and revolutionary depth strengthened my understanding of the value of unconditional love in my life. Unconditional love, at its core, is an adoration free of circumstances and unconnected to feelings. It necessitates empathy for the ideas, feelings, and worldviews of individuals you interact with. This love is founded on compassion, the ability to empathize with and grasp another person's feelings and sorrow. Because of my ability to empathize with others, my relationships with the people I care about are reinforced, and we get closer. Because I can empathize, I can put myself in their shoes and understand their feelings and experiences.

Compassion, on the other hand, is a dynamic manifestation of empathy. Helping someone means taking action to improve their situation. Giving without expecting anything in return comes easy to someone with an unconditionally loving heart. It inspires me to be there for people through their most difficult times, providing them a secure environment to express themselves and comfort in my company. I'm inspired to help, to offer encouraging words, or to listen with compassion because I know my concern and empathy can make a difference in their lives.

Compassion and empathy have a far-reaching impact on my ability to cultivate unconditional love that stretches beyond my relationships. A sense of belonging and tranquillity may flourish when I approach my relationships with empathy and a desire to know the other person's point of view and experiences. As my capacity to empathize has developed, I can now better perceive and understand the differences between people.

I appreciate donating to others and aiding underprivileged communities, even when not benefiting me directly. When viewed through the perspective of compassion, unconditional love encourages me to serve others and participate in projects to make our world a better place. When I help those in need, whether via humanitarian work or relief efforts after natural disasters, my compassion and drive to make the world a better place grows.

I've learned the significance of unconditional love through empathy and compassion. Consequently, my connections with family, friends, and coworkers strengthen, and I feel supported and valued. It has motivated me to make a positive difference for the greater good and has helped me feel more at ease in the world. I can live a meaningful and worthwhile life motivated by care and regard for others because unconditional love, formed through empathy and compassion, is a guiding concept that defines my character and decisions.

Learning the importance of unconditional love has been a journey of continuing self-awareness and progress for me, made richer by the ongoing roles of compassion and empathy. I've realized that unconditional love is more than just a feeling; it's also a decision and a way of being. It necessitates an accepting mentality that welcomes the flaws and defects that make us human. I may make a basic connection with folks by seeing past visible differences and building a common understanding.

Because of empathy, I've learned to listen to people without criticizing them or feeling obligated to find solutions to their difficulties. Instead, I provide my kind presence, which includes encouragement and support. This realization strengthens my connections with the individuals I care about and lays the groundwork for mutual respect, trust, and honesty.

Because of empathy, I've formed long-lasting relationships with others.

Empathy develops compassion, and compassion motivates me to step in and provide a helping hand when I see others hurting or going through a difficult moment. It allows me to help individuals in need by giving them strength and hope. When I'm empathetic, I can put my concerns aside and focus on those of others. It encourages me to assist individuals in need whenever possible, whether by lending a hand, donating resources, or simply listening.

Unconditional love, empathy, and compassion are all intertwined values that have taught me to be patient and understand myself. It is a constant reminder that I, too, deserve compassion, forgiveness, and love. Because of self-compassion, I can accept my flaws and be as kind and forgiving to myself as I am to others. Self-compassion has helped me let go of harsh judgment of myself and learn to love and accept myself precisely as I am.

As I strive to enhance my capacity for empathy and compassion, unconditional love begins taking on greater relevance in my life as a guiding idea. As a result, my approach to dispute resolution has shifted since I now prioritize understanding above winning. As a result, I am motivated to work for a more equal and caring society.

The unconditional love I cultivate via empathy and compassion is more powerful than the relationships of my closest pals. This is why it is critical to be polite and kind to strangers. People may spread unconditional love over the entire earth by being kind to one another and working together to better the globe.

In the end, unconditional love is inextricably related to empathy and compassion. These three characteristics influence how I connect with others, make decisions, and live my life. I may find solace in my relationships with others, embrace the ups and downs of human existence, and believe in the force of kindness inside us. I'm learning the importance of unconditional love as I go, and it's preparing me for a life full of meaning, empathy, and compassion.

Tolerance, compassion, and forbearance may all contribute significantly to the survival of love in challenging circumstances. When confronted with difficult circumstances, it is common for individuals to experience emotional anguish and engage in abusive discourse. When individuals in a relationship demonstrate approval and non-judgment toward one another, their responses and the issue may shift significantly.

When two individuals have affection for one another, they tolerate one another's faults and defects. The concept entails embracing and appreciating people's inherent humanity and responsibilities and comprehending and valuing diversity. When individuals in a relationship can let go of unrealistic expectations and benchmarks, their relationship has the potential to evolve into a state that is more genuine and authentic.

Similar to acceptance, non-judgment can assist couples in navigating challenging situations by reducing evaluative or accusatory language. Before rushing to conclusions or making unfounded assumptions, it is essential to devote sufficient time to active listening. Establishing trust and a sense of safety within relationships through open and inclusive communication enables participants to express their problems, perspectives, and ideas without fear of being negatively evaluated.

Acceptance and non-judgment, especially in difficult situations, can prevent arguments from devolving into toxic habits. Rather than acting defensively or antagonistically against one another, partners focus on understanding one another's perspectives and needs. If they accept and respect one another's feelings, they can work together to develop solutions and compromises that are fair to both parties.

Couples that embrace this viewpoint are more likely to look beyond current difficulties and reignite their passion over a shared love and commitment. Their shared understanding that they all deserve to be treated with acceptance and without judgment enhances their resolve to assist and promote one another.

If you adopt an accepting and nonjudgmental attitude, you can gain understanding and perspective from difficult circumstances. The couples have a better grasp of their emotional responses and what causes them. Partners who have acquired this level of self-awareness are better able to communicate and meet the needs of their partners, as well as be compassionate toward themselves when times are rough.

Furthermore, having a nonjudgmental and welcoming attitude allows individuals to forgive and let go of grudges. Instead of harboring bitterness or obsessing over past wrongs, partners practice forgiveness and living in the present. This ability for forgiveness may aid in the growth and strengthening of the connection.

Finally, an acceptance and nonjudgmental attitude fosters a strong and understanding connection, which is required to retain love during challenging conditions. Couples can manage difficult circumstances together if they are reassured that their love and support will not change. You may deepen your relationship and raise the possibility that your love will withstand hardship by tackling difficulties in this manner. A loving and caring relationship may be maintained through life's ups and downs with the help of acceptance and non-judgment on both sides.

Partners may actively work on increasing emotional closeness and vulnerability by developing an attitude of acceptance and non-judgment. Talking freely and honestly about how you're feeling and what you're going through is critical when challenges grow. Both partners deserve a comfortable environment where they may open up to one another about their flaws and anxieties without fear of rejection or criticism.

Through communication on such a personal level, partners can better understand, appreciate, and empathize with one another. They know the potential psychological strain that adversity may place on their connection. They strengthen their friendship and sense of solidarity by acknowledging the genuineness of one another's ideas and being aware that they are not facing challenges on their own.

Adversity can make couples stronger when they face it with acceptance and non-judgment toward one another. They put an end to pointing fingers at one another and take collective responsibility for finding solutions and weathering the storm. Through working together, they are building their camaraderie and coming to terms with the idea that they are in this together, providing each other with encouragement and support.

In addition, cultivating an attitude of acceptance and non-judgment can make it much easy for you to see and value the positive aspects of your connection with the other person. Partners eventually discover how to recognize and encourage one another's efforts to deal with challenging circumstances. When one person expresses gratitude to another, it often creates a domino effect of more expressions of appreciation and respect.

When going through challenging circumstances, partners often share moments that are vulnerable to them both emotionally and physically. They can maintain a tolerant and nonjudgmental outlook, enabling them to view times of vulnerability as opportunities for growth and development. They are aware that being emotionally vulnerable with one another and trusting one another in difficult circumstances is not a sign of weakness but rather of strength in their relationship.

A mindset of accepting others and not judging them is valuable beyond the realm of difficulties. It becomes a way of life for the couple, and it impacts how they manage the ups and downs of their experience together. When one partner consistently demonstrates acceptance and nonjudgmental behavior toward the other in their interactions, their love and connection grow deeper.

It is nearly impossible to place an adequate amount of emphasis on the significance of maintaining love in the face of adversity by adopting a nonjudgmental attitude. This approach fosters an emotional connection between spouses and respect and empathy for one another as these qualities are developed. A healthy relationship requires both parties to be willing to be vulnerable with one another and to accept the shortcomings of the other. They remain hopeful in the face of adversity, help one another out when one is in need, and grow as a group. The love that develops between partners who make an effort to be accepting of one another and refrain from passing judgment on one another can endure challenges and ensures that they will always be there for one another to offer solace and assistance.

Chapter 11: Understanding Modern Romance in the Age of Technology

I'm amazed at how much influence contemporary technology, such as the Internet and other platforms, has had on our love meetings. The principles of love have shifted with the development of instant messaging, dating apps, and Internet communication. Face-to-face dating and courting have given way to online discussions and introductions. The ease with which possible spouses may be found today is astounding. It just takes a few screen taps. However, its usage could be improved. Even while technology brings people closer together, true emotions may be buried in the world of texts and emoticons, leading to feelings of detachment and superficiality.

Many options in dating apps may create a paradox of choice, making settling down and engaging in a committed relationship more difficult. This is correct, but technological advancements like video calling and instant messaging have made it simpler for long-distance couples to stay connected over time. Because teams can instantaneously exchange experiences, ideas, and feelings with one another, romantic relationships seem more immediate today. However, since honesty and openness in a two-person relationship are key to romance, it's critical to establish a balance between online and in-person interaction. It is possible to navigate contemporary romance thoughtfully and meaningfully in the computer age by enjoying its advantages while being aware of its potential pitfalls.

I notice how the internet world is changing how we meet possible companions and connect with and show our love for one another. Couples may now instantaneously communicate their ideas, emotions, and experiences with one another thanks to texting and other forms of digital communication. Communication accessibility has undeniably benefited relationships, bringing individuals together and making them feel more accessible than ever before.

Furthermore, thanks to current technology, we may rapidly express our joy when we achieve major or little life milestones. Couples may form a stronger link due to the ability to share voice messages, videos, and images. Celebrating birthdays, anniversaries, and solemn dedications in public has grown more common in internet situations. This technology feature has surely enhanced love expression by allowing couples to share their emotions freely and building a sense of community among those in similar relationships.

However, we must not disregard technological limitations. Couples may spend more time with their electronics than with one another due to modern conveniences such as continual connection. Having a vast online buddy network may cause you to assume you are closer than you are. Modern couples must balance digital activities with quality time spent together in person to create a stronger emotional relationship with their partner.

The rise of social networking sites has also generated several obstacles for contemporary love stories. Individuals who compare their love lives online may feel inadequate and resentful of others. Privacy concerns are also highlighted by the possibility of disclosing sensitive information about people's connections to a large audience.

To summarize, it is undeniable that contemporary technology has revolutionized romantic relationships by opening up previously unimaginable channels of contact and intimacy. It has helped couples keep in touch despite their separation and find new methods to show their love for one another. However, we must utilize technology wisely, be aware of its hazards, and seek to keep real emotions and genuine human relationships at the heart of our love encounters. We must balance technology's advantages and authentic face-to-face engagement to develop long-lasting, meaningful connections in the digital age.

The fast growth of technology is bringing even more interesting changes to the current romantic environment. Virtual reality (VR) and augmented reality (AR) are potential methods for improving communication in long-distance relationships. Couples may feel closer by experiencing being together when separated in virtual reality (VR). A deeper, limitless relationship may be formed by participating in digital activities such as "virtual dates," "virtual world exploration," or spending time in each other's digital company.

Furthermore, the rise of AI has begun to take centre stage in contemporary love stories. Artificial intelligence is assisting dating applications in better-matching users based on their shared interests, beliefs, and hobbies. Chatbots with natural language processing skills have been developed to recreate human-like discussions to assist further folks who feel lonely in the digital world.

Regardless of these possible new developments, caution is suggested. Concerns about privacy and safety are rising as relationships, and technology become more intertwined. Concerns regarding data privacy and abuse have been expressed due to the large amounts of personal information made accessible through applications and social media sites. Furthermore, the ease with which people can form connections online exposes them to fraud, abuse, and catfishing risks.

While there is no doubt that contemporary dating apps have their benefits, it is important to remember the value of true human connection and emotional closeness. The advantages of modern technology and the importance of genuine human connection must coexist. Couples should establish limits and ensure that their online interactions supplement rather than replace in-person conversations.

Modern technology has surely altered the way we see and pursue love relationships. From the ease of online dating to the immersion of virtual reality and the support of AI companions, modern relationships are becoming more dependent on technology. By being deliberate about how we use digital technologies, we may use them to improve and deepen our love relationships without jeopardizing the openness and honesty that serve as the core of successful partnerships. Understanding of contemporary romance in the digital era will grow as technology progresses.

There are thrilling prospects and significant impediments to romance in the digital era. Fortunately, there are several ways that modern technology may help couples improve their bonds and keep the fire burning in their marriages. Despite the physical distance, teams may communicate via IM and video calling throughout the day. We may still record and celebrate great moments despite our physical separation by sharing photographs, videos, and voice messages. The increased usage of social media allows for public declarations of love and sharing of pleasant milestones such as anniversaries and other special celebrations. The simplicity of social networking and dating services has increased the number of potential partners one may encounter. The Internet provides many options for modern couples to stay in touch, maintain and improve their emotional connection.

Despite these benefits, there may be some drawbacks. One major issue is that society will become too dependent on technology, separating people and their environment. Constant online communication may unintentionally diminish the importance of face-to-face contact and physical touch, both necessary for forming a strong relationship. Because they want to offer an idealized image of their relationship online, some couples may experience feelings of inadequacy or jealousy due to their use of social media. People may feel anxious or dissatisfied due to the digital world's rapid speed; more options and faster responses to requests may also heighten expectations. The true heart of romance should be preserved in the digital appeal; a good balance of online and offline encounters should exist.

Finally, the conveniences of the digital era have enabled contemporary relationships to keep romanticism in several ways. Couples' emotional bonds may be strengthened via instant messaging, virtual date nights, and online friendships with individuals who share their interests. Nevertheless, traversing these digital places with caution and knowledge is essential. Excessive reliance on technology has been linked to the promotion of feelings of inadequacy and unhappiness due to online comparisons and a decrease in interpersonal connection and authenticity. Couples may benefit from the digital age while keeping their relationship's basis by stressing emotional closeness and using technology to enhance rather than replace in-person encounters.

The importance of maintaining romantic relationships is heightened by the abundance of information and services available to us nowadays. Online resources abound for couples seeking advice on improving their relationships, improving communication channels, and reigniting the romance after many years of marriage. Teams may benefit from online lectures and seminars on the five love languages, conflict resolution, and emotional intelligence. Partners who participate in online discussion boards and support groups may feel a feeling of kinship and support while obtaining advice from others who have been through similar experiences.

Technology has also simplified the planning and execution of romantic surprises and gestures. Partners may brighten one other's day by organizing a surprise delivery of presents, flowers, or handwritten messages using various apps and services. Couples may now pursue hobbies like cooking, watching films or playing games together even if they are in separate regions, thanks to the increasing usage of video conferencing technology. These unconventional dating techniques may bring new life into a relationship by bringing intrigue and variety.

On the other hand, technology may interfere with private discussions. Priceless moments of connecting may be lost due to distractions such as constant alarms, social media browsing, and the belief that one must constantly be online. Even though they are physically near, couples who spend too much time alone with their technology gadgets may feel alone and distant.

Furthermore, the simplicity of texting and talking might lead to tone misunderstandings or misinterpretations, resulting in unneeded confrontations or bad sentiments. More care and attention are required to ensure digital communication stays respectful, empathetic, and clear since verbal and nonverbal clues may be lost without face-to-face conversations.

To summarize, dating in the digital era offers many benefits. When partners access knowledge, internet tools, and virtual experiences, they may develop a deeper mutual understanding and a stronger emotional attachment. Technology may assist a relationship by giving romantic surprises and gestures that keep things exciting and entertaining between partners. However, there are problems to be aware of, such as technology diversions and digital misunderstandings. Achieving a mix of in-person and online interactions will assist married people in maintaining strong relationships in the modern digital world.

Developing lasting connections in today's digital world takes deliberate effort. Genuine relationships should always be prioritized over forged ones. Although it takes effort to get to know someone better, technology makes it simple and fast to have fun. Engaging in meaningful discussions, asking thought-provoking questions, and paying attention to one another may provide the groundwork for a more genuine connection.

Maintaining a healthy mix of online and offline activities is also critical. Even though electronic communication tools may lessen physical barriers to interaction, it is best to use them in addition to, rather than as a substitute for, personal meetings.

Spending time together away from electronics may help you get to know each other better and deepen your emotional connection.

Having clear limits is crucial in the digital sphere. Setting limitations on screen time and designating tech-free hours may help couples be completely present for one another in a world where it's easy to get caught up in the continual stream of messages and social media updates. Consequently, when they are together, they become more sensitive to one another and communicate more profoundly.

Furthermore, real and truthful communication is more important in the digital age than ever. Honest communication regarding hopes, worries, and emotions is required to promote openness, trust, and understanding. Technology should assist communication rather than obstruct conflict resolution, and any difficulties that emerge should be addressed quickly and respectfully.

Even in this day and age of instant gratification, it is important to enjoy the little things. Sending a handwritten letter, making an unexpected video call, or sharing digital memories may all make someone feel special and treasured. Even the smallest acts of kindness can deepen connections and have a long-lasting impact on those who see them.

Finally, one of the finest ways to strengthen your relationship is having common hobbies and experiences. Take online classes, play games, or even organize virtual trips to enhance your connection with your significant other while having fun.

To summarise, developing genuine connections in the modern digital environment requires focus, honesty, and a balance of online and offline hobbies. In the digital era, promoting real connections, setting clear limits, and savoring the tiny moments may lead to stronger emotional attachments and more meaningful and long-lasting relationships.

Maintaining meaningful interactions in today's digital environment requires careful consideration of the content we consume and share online. What we see on social media may alter our perceptions of ourselves and others, making it a double-edged sword. Transparency and trust should be fostered to create communities where people feel safe being themselves online.

Moreover, genuine concern and attention for one another greatly help form good interpersonal relationships. Even though the Internet may sometimes be cold and impersonal, telling a stranger that you care, even if just online, can significantly impact their lives. Small, thoughtful activities such as mailing encouraging letters during difficult times or celebrating one another's triumphs may reveal a strong emotional bond.

Understanding and patience are necessary in today's fast-paced digital environment. It's important to remember that building solid connections takes time and work, so there's no need to rush or put pressure on them to grow quickly. Building trust, emotional connection, and mutual understanding results in more meaningful and satisfying relationships.

Respect and decency should be maintained during online conversations by using digital etiquette. By being conscious of our words, abstaining from using them, and not oversharing personal information, we may foster a pleasant and helpful online community that develops connections.

It is also vital to be willing to experiment with cutting-edge means of connecting and exchanging information in today's digital environment. Shared playlists, online games, and virtual reality (VR) experiences may all add excitement and novelty to a relationship while also encouraging risk-taking and strengthening bonds via a shared enjoyment of a shared passion.

Finally, it is vital to recognize contemporary technology's limitations and problems. It's critical to stay cheerful and patient when dealing with technology glitches, misunderstandings, and other forms of digital alienation. By accepting these inherent flaws in the digital experience, couples can focus on what matters most: their emotional connection and the delight of being together.

To summarize, making long-lasting connections in today's digital environment involves a combination of intention, empathy, and adaptability. In the evolving digital world, one may build long-lasting and meaningful relationships by valuing real connections, encouraging open communication, and adopting digital etiquette. Relationships in the digital era may be more rewarding and authentic if people are aware of the effects of technology and use the opportunities it provides.

Because today's interactions must be enjoyable and healthy, creating and maintaining digital boundaries is critical. As technology permeates every part of our lives, it is easy to ignore the importance of cultivating offline contacts. To protect the integrity of our relationships and ensure that technology improves rather than detracts from our emotional closeness, we must establish clear digital boundaries with our partners. These constraints may include refraining from using gadgets when engaging in activities like dining together or having sexually explicit chats and exercising caution while making internet posts about our relationship. Maintaining these limits indicates your dedication to building trusting relationships and always remaining present with your spouse. Furthermore, respecting one another's digital borders, we can maintain a healthy balance of our online and offline experiences. Setting and sticking to clear digital boundaries may be the key to maintaining successful relationships in the digital age.

Setting and maintaining digital boundaries can protect our relationships' quality and mental and emotional well-being. The continual flood of information, social comparisons, and the need to always be present in the digital world can contribute to emotions of stress, anxiety, and even inadequacy. If we restrict the amount of time we spend on digital devices, we can better care for one another and ourselves without being continuously bombarded with information accessible online.

Creating digital boundaries may also aid in the prevention of arguments and misunderstandings. Because nonverbal indicators are missing in online talks, they might lead to misunderstandings and damaged sentiments. We may avoid unwittingly aggravating the situation by being courteous in our messaging and creating ground rules for our online connections.

Maintaining reasonable boundaries for your online connections may help you remember that you are more important than your screens. It demonstrates that we value our partner's presence and participation in our life and relationship over the continual enticement of social media or digital entertainment. This mutual respect and dedication develop the partnership's emotional connection and foundation.

Furthermore, we may preserve a good work-life balance by imposing digital boundaries. The ubiquity of mobile devices and constant interaction blurs the barriers between our personal and work lives. Setting strong limits on how often and when you check business emails and texts allows you to spend quality time with your spouse without being distracted by work difficulties.

Finally, there are several compelling reasons why it is critical to establish and maintain digital boundaries in today's interactions. When we prioritize one another over technology distractions, we protect our relationships' quality and mental and emotional health. We prepare for true friendships to thrive in the digital era by establishing these limits. It reflects how seriously we take our marriage and how devoted we are to maintaining harmony despite technology's pervasiveness in our everyday lives.

Setting and maintaining digital boundaries in interpersonal interactions is becoming increasingly important in a technologically advanced culture. Couples who consistently keep these boundaries may create a deeper feeling of mutual respect for one another's privacy and personal space requirements. This shared experience creates an emotionally safe space where both people may be honest and transparent about their vulnerabilities without fear of cyber-invasion.

As a bonus, erecting virtual walls may aid partners in focusing on their progress and well-being. Partners may be better able to support one another's interests and passions if they set apart time and space free of technology. This promotes independence and personal growth while widening the couple's mutual interests and discussion subjects.

Couples who set reasonable limits for their internet relationships may be great role models for their friends and family. The beneficial effects of these limits on the connection may inspire other close friends and family members to try them. If more individuals realize the importance of digital boundaries, there may be a cultural change toward more deliberate and aware digital interactions in various social circumstances.

Setting digital boundaries can also assist couples in having open and productive communication. Couples who discuss and agree on these boundaries may better understand one another's needs, views, and concerns about technology. You can learn more about each other's preferences and develop limits appropriate for your relationship by negotiating and compromising.

Finally, preserving a virtual and physical distance may allow couples to spend more time and energy together. Maintaining these limits encourages couples to devote time and energy to making experiences that will enhance their relationship over time, whether trying out a new pastime, going on a trip, or simply talking without interruptions.

Finally, creating and maintaining digital boundaries not only aids in the survival of modern relationships but also builds trust, intimacy, and openness between partners. Couples may live in harmony in the digital era by maintaining these limits and developing ties based on emotional closeness, mutual respect, and a shared desire for self-improvement. Accepting digital restrictions is essential for managing the quickly changing technological world while keeping the basics of meaningful and successful interactions.

When communicating through technology in a love relationship, honesty and trust are two of the most important factors. These characteristics are especially important in today's world, as people are increasingly inclined to interact through digital means. When two people can communicate honestly and openly with one another, they create a safe place in which they may share their deepest ideas and feelings.

Honesty in online communication necessitates telling the truth and expressing our true feelings and motivations. When communicating via text or social media, it is critical to communicate openly and honestly. Being honest about your sentiments is critical
 because nonverbal indicators aren't always there.

Trustworthiness and honesty go hand in hand in the digital era; both are required for success. Feeling safe in a digital connection requires trust in participants' sincerity and transparency. When we know that our spouse will respect our space and feelings, we can be genuinely honest and truthful.

Our degree of trust in a social media partner influences how we interact with their online presence. Intimacy and trust may weaken when one spouse gets into the other's digital life. Feeling safe and comfortable in a relationship necessitates trusting that one's partner will respect one's personal space and digital boundaries.

When dealing with challenges caused by internet engagement, honesty and trust go a long way. Conflicts may be resolved and avoided if people are willing to discuss their problems openly and honestly. If we are certain that our spouse has our best interests at heart, we can approach these talks with a collaborative mindset and a willingness to work together to find answers.

To summarize, utilizing technology for romantic communication may be beneficial, but only if done honestly and truthfully. Doing so creates an environment where both parties may express themselves honestly and openly online. Couples that adhere to these rules will be better able to deal with the rigours of modern communication, resulting in a stronger emotional connection and a longer-lasting relationship.

When utilizing technology for romantic communication, honesty and trustworthiness are continual actions that need deliberate attention. As technology brings new difficulties and possibilities, partners must regularly review their digital boundaries and communication patterns.

Regular communication and an open conversation about the topic can assist in mitigating the negative effects of technology on a relationship. Partners can work together to solve any difficulties or concerns that have occurred as a result of digital communication. Giving and receiving honest feedback about how each individual feels in cyberspace might help uncover problem areas and develop a higher level of emotional closeness.

Taking each other's personal space and communication preferences into account is crucial for creating trusted online interactions. One partner should respect the other's decision and not feel compelled to reveal specific relationship details online if they so choose. Respecting these limits promotes individuality while increasing reliance on one's spouse.

It's also important to remember that conversing online might lead to misunderstandings and disagreements. It's easy to misinterpret the tone of a text message, which might lead to an awkward encounter. To avoid avoidable confrontation, it is critical to give each other the benefit of the doubt, seek clarity rather than presuming and retain trust.

Furthermore, building confidence online necessitates the use of proper digital ways. Even in the digital realm, acting with attention and concern for our partner's feelings demonstrates that we value our relationship.

Taking the time to appreciate contemporary technology's unique opportunities is one of the most underrated ways a couple's connection may be strengthened. It's possible that enjoying technology-facilitated moments of connection, like a surprise video call or a virtual date night, might make the romantic encounter more enjoyable.

Partners may use digital platforms to accomplish major things together and enjoy the moments of connection made possible by technology. If you wish to build the intellectual links that bind you to others, consider trading articles, movies, or podcasts on subjects of mutual interest with another person. Working together virtually on projects like vacation planning, photo albums, or artistic works can help people feel more connected to one another and a common goal.

Technology also gives long-distance couples a special opportunity to bring the space between them closer while keeping their connection. Video calling and instant messaging have allowed teams to spend entire days together, go on "virtual date nights," and even watch movies or read books simultaneously. Long-distance couples who share these common experiences may feel as though they are physically closer to one another than they are.

Even if we recognize and appreciate the benefits of technology, we still need to use it thoughtfully and deliberately. It is essential to strike a healthy equilibrium between in-person and virtual interactions to maintain the connection's authenticity and breadth. It could benefit the emotional connections that partners have with one another if they put away their technological gadgets and spend more time together.

In conclusion, strengthening the link between partners may be accomplished by actively participating in meaningful digital activities and embracing the special advantages technology brings to the relationship.

Enhancing the romantic experience and contributing to enduring memories can be aided by commemorating intimate events and using technology to circumvent geographical limitations. Maintaining a healthy balance of online and offline communication is essential when it comes to keeping a relationship reliable and truthful. Couples who work together to conquer the digital world have a better chance of building a love that lasts both online and off.

Using technology for romantic connection significantly emphasizes the upkeep of established standards of honesty and trust. Having open talks, respecting each other's limitations, and being aware of proper digital etiquette are ways partners may build confidence in the digital sphere. Suppose both parties are willing to embrace the great features of technology while being open and calm about discussing the negative aspects. In that case, relationships have a higher chance of flourishing and adapting to the modern digital environment.

Chapter 12: Loving others and oneself: laying the groundwork

Chapter 12 focuses extensively on the pivotal significance of self-love in fostering profound interpersonal relationships. It has been recognized that cultivating a strong sense of self-worth and empathy toward oneself is a prerequisite for establishing enduring interpersonal connections. When individuals embrace their true selves, including their imperfections, they are likelier to engage in partnerships characterized by sincerity and emotional equilibrium. The cultivation of self-love contributes to the promotion of compassion, empathy, and benevolence toward others. The reservoir of faith enables individuals to give and receive love, respect, and support without compromising their welfare.

Ultimately, to cultivate enduring and harmonious relationships founded upon reciprocal regard, reliance, and empathy, we must acquire the ability to embrace ourselves. This analysis delves further into the intricate interplay between self-affection and the capacity to cultivate robust interpersonal connections. To establish successful partnerships with others, we must go on a journey of self-exploration and self-acceptance. The cultivation of self-love may be achieved via the development of self-awareness, whereby individuals can see their strengths and weaknesses objectively. Individuals can foster a genuine sense of self-love by acknowledging and accepting these imperfections with grace and compassion. Enhancing our comprehension and establishing meaningful connections with others may be facilitated by cultivating self-kindness.

One of the benefits of increasing self-awareness is the capacity to detect better the emotions of others with whom we engage. This self-love-born empathy allows us to negotiate the complexities of human emotion more effectively, opening the door for open dialogue and trust. Knowing and appreciating our value will enable us to assist and encourage others without risking our well-being.

Self-love keeps you from falling into the codependency trap or continually looking to others for approval. When we know our value, we no longer need to seek acceptance from others eagerly. With increased self-assurance, we may lay aside preconceived notions about how relationships should work to focus on what makes the other person happy.

Cultivating self-love opens the door to a rich tapestry of interactions characterized by reciprocal compassion and admiration. When we prioritize ourselves and learn to respect who we are, our relationships with others improve. This chapter vividly demonstrates that we can only love others after learning to love and care for ourselves.

Through this process of self-examination, we may tear down the boundaries that have prevented us from making meaningful relationships with others. As we get more comfortable with our flaws, we can better be empathetic and sympathetic toward people different from us. True relationships may blossom when we learn to love ourselves, which bridges our inner and outside lives.

Self-love is a source of emotional sturdiness in and of itself. When we make an effort to build a good connection with ourselves, we get the inner strength we need to cope with the obstacles that arise in other relationships. When we don't give in to emotions of shame or inadequacy, we can articulate our expectations more effectively, create appropriate limits, and speak more clearly. This mental toughness benefits not just our personal lives but also our interpersonal connections.

This chapter tells us how self-love may liberate us from the destructive cycles of rivalry and comparison. When we are at ease in our skin, we become less sensitive to the achievements and virtues of others around us. Instead, we may encourage one another by publicly congratulating one another on their successes.

Self-love is a vivid thread that threads through all of your interpersonal connections. As a result, we may love, listen closely without judgment, and be there for those we care about. When we take care of ourselves, we provide the groundwork for genuine, compassionate, and respectful connections with others. This chapter urges us to go on a journey of self-discovery that will enrich our lives by demonstrating the fundamental relationship between self-love and other people.

The journey of learning to love myself and others more profoundly has been both life-changing and illuminating. The first stage is introspection—willing to go into the depths of my thoughts, feelings, and experiences. Self-acceptance is the foundation upon which self-love is built, and I achieved self-acceptance by totally accepting myself, warts and all. This experience has taught me the importance of self-compassion, self-care, and health maintenance.

Love for me has significantly influenced how I interact with others. It's as if a door has been opened to greater awareness of and connection with the world around me and self-compassion. By attentively listening to other people's points of view and putting myself in other people's shoes, I've learnt the value of empathy in developing and sustaining successful relationships.

My gratitude practice has immediately expanded my ability to love. It has assisted me in seeing the value and beauty in each person to see the best in myself and others. We now feel closer to one another and appreciate the time we spend together.

Learning to love myself fully and others take time and effort. It requires being there for the people in my life, letting down my guard, and actively finding opportunities to help and encourage them. Finally, this journey has benefited my life in unfathomable ways by allowing me to create connections with open, empathic, and sincere individuals in their love.

Learning to love oneself and others more profoundly has been a tremendous and never-ending journey of discovery. It's a voyage of self-discovery that requires much introspection and self-compassion. Due to my investigation of my mental landscape, my underlying motivations, experiences, and character attributes have become more evident. Accepting one's worth has become a cornerstone of self-love, enabling me to cherish my individuality while keeping a positive self-image.

The marvel of this experience is how it will affect my interactions with others. I've discovered a bigger reservoir of empathy and a stronger sense of human connection thanks to self-compassion and self-acceptance. When I allow myself to embrace my own experience completely, my capacity to connect to the experiences of others has been reawakened. I've been able to communicate with others more honestly and freely due to this empathy, which has enhanced my relationships with the individuals I care about.

Mindfulness meditation has significantly improved my capacity to love. When I maintain my focus in the present, I can better participate in talks and pay close attention to what other people are saying and experiencing. A deeper bond is formed when someone is there based on true understanding and mutual support.

The capacity to love oneself and others is something that one works on throughout their life. It's a journey that requires perseverance, adaptation, and a good attitude in the face of adversity. This experience has taught me that the more self-love I cultivate, the more I have to give the world. The dance between loving myself and loving others has significantly improved my life by transforming my interactions with others into enormous sources of pleasure and happiness.

My journey to learn how to love myself and others more fully is intertwined with reflection, sensitivity, and a persistent will to evolve. This journey starts with an introspective examination of the complex network of thoughts, values, and emotions that comprise my self. I've done this because it has helped me accept and cherish all aspects of my personality, from my strengths to my flaws. A flame of self-love ignited by this accepting understanding has enhanced my connections with others.

As I go down this path, my ability for empathy and compassion for others grows dramatically. When I utilize my own life experiences to understand the achievements and disappointments of the people I deal with, kindness becomes a powerful elixir that deepens bonds. Because I love myself, I can empathize with others and be there for them when they need support, encouragement, or someone to listen.

My search for a deeper love connection necessitates a reflective attitude. It's a practice that keeps me in the current moment, allowing me to interact completely with people around me rather than stressing about the past or the future. Because of mindfulness's lessons on embracing the ephemeral, priceless

239

moments that make up the tapestry of shared experiences, I can now give more of myself to my relationships.

Through this process, I've realized that love is a resource that can be refilled; the more I invest in it, the more it grows and flows into my relationships. It's a virtuous circle in which loving myself more fully strengthens my capacity to love others, resulting in a beautiful symphony of interwoven souls. This road of self-examination, compassion, and awareness has illuminated the complicated relationship between self-love and the tremendous attachment we may have for the people who make our lives full.

My connection with myself has improved tremendously due to my participation in self-love and self-care activities and exercises. I've acquired the practice of using daily affirmations. When I look in the mirror in the morning, I talk to myself in an encouraging tone. Claims such as "I am capable," "I am worthy," and "I deserve love" have become a salve for my spirit, serving as a constant source of confidence and a reminder of my worth.

I've also mentioned writing as a relaxing activity. Because of this activity, I can think more clearly, evaluate my emotions more thoroughly, and get insight into my inner self. Journaling has proven therapeutic for me, whether I'm scribbling down my sentiments and thoughts about what occurred that day, reflecting on the lessons I've learned, or creating goals for the future.

I describe self-love as taking excellent care of my body via exercise and a healthy diet. When I take care of my body via exercise and nutritious eating, I feel more energetic and joyous and better medically. This investment in myself is an act of self-love since it demonstrates how much I respect and care about my general health and well-being.

When I needed it the most, mindfulness and meditation provided a safe sanctuary of tranquillity. I can tune out the outer world through meditation, prayer, and contemplation and hear what my soul is trying to tell me. Mindfulness activities such as meditation and deep breathing have enhanced my capacity to stay calm and focused in adversity.

Finally, the path to self-love and self-care is extremely individualized, tailored to my circumstances and tastes. Through persistent practice, I've woven a tapestry of self-compassion that feeds my spirit and creates a strong feeling of self-connection.

I've included numerous previously impossible events into my daily routine by prioritizing my pleasure and wellness. Keeping a gratitude notebook has continually inspired me. I reflect on the day's events every night before bed and jot down my appreciation. Finding and appreciating the good elements of my life influences my attitude and generates a feeling of contentment.

Making art is another fantastic way to appreciate oneself. Expressing my unique blend of strengths and interests is advantageous via creative undertakings such as writing, painting, and music-making. I tell my feelings, organize my ideas, and enjoy being myself via my artistic side.

Spending time in nature has proven to be refreshing for me. I always feel invigorated and more connected to the world after spending time in nature, whether a quiet walk through a park or a strenuous mountain climb. Nature's serenity serves as a subconscious reminder to take a moment to breathe deeply and show gratitude.

Another step toward self-love is learning to be sympathetic and forgiving of oneself. I've learned to treat myself with the same patience and care as others. I remember that I am human and that obstacles and flaws are expected in this life. Through self-compassion training, I've learned to let go of critical beliefs about myself and replace them with kinder, more understanding ones.

When feeling apprehensive, I use relaxation tactics like taking a warm bath or deep breathing exercises. These peaceful times serve as a subtle reminder to pause and recharge.

Self-love and pursuing activities that foster it have evolved into an everyday ritual. My self-awareness and caring for myself are intricately interwoven because of the many strategies I use.

After serious consideration, I've concluded that developing a healthy sense of psychological well-being and a deep, abiding love for one's own person requires a solid foundation in self-awareness. The complex inner workings of one's mind and behaviour may be better understood via self-awareness. This introspection has helped me see my areas of excellence, weaknesses, and triggers.

This realization has helped me start developing healthy self-esteem. As I have come to accept and appreciate all of my unique qualities, so has expanded my capacity for self-compassion. This is not a shallow affection; it comes from a deep appreciation of who I am and the recognition that I am worthy of being loved and cared for, flaws and all.

Training in self-awareness is also an excellent method for enhancing emotional well-being. Through introspection, I've learned to keep my rational mind apart from my emotional one. I can now confront life's challenges confidently and clearly because of my acquired knowledge. I'm in a better place emotionally now that I've identified and addressed my emotional triggers and destructive thought patterns.

Self-love and, more generally, mental health is built on the bedrock of self-awareness. By examining our inner lives, we are freed from the expectations of others and may unconditionally accept who we are. The more I discover who I am, the more confident I am in creating a life filled with true love, harmonious relationships, and deep satisfaction.

When one considers the interconnected nature of love and psychological well-being, the value of introspection becomes abundantly evident. Along my journey of self-discovery, I've learned to value self-awareness for the bridge it provides between my cerebral reasoning and my unconscious emotions and habits. Awakening has given me the clarity of mind to more easily navigate the maze of my mind.

I needed to get rid of any mental roadblocks that were preventing me from loving myself without conditions. I uncovered the part of myself that deserves to be treated with love and respect by letting go of ideas and cultural expectations. With this insight comes a deep and abiding appreciation for the complex mosaic of traits that makes up my unique identity.

Maintaining an equilibrium between mental well-being and self-awareness is challenging. As a consequence of my increased self-awareness, I can now pinpoint the causes of my emotional ups and downs. This insight has enabled me to practice mindfulness and other coping techniques that help me maintain emotional stability. As a result, they are emotionally stronger, happier with themselves, and better able to deal with the stresses of daily life.

As a consequence, the path to self-awareness becomes a life-changing experience that results in a more compassionate and psychologically nourishing you. I've realized that the deeper I delve inside, the more wisdom, compassion, and acceptance I find. This exercise allows me to feel more connected to myself, others, and the rest of the world. In reality, a life distinguished by a deep connection and a good mental state is based on a solid foundation of self-awareness.

When we examine how self-awareness influences personal development and one's capacity to form meaningful relationships with others, the necessity of being aware of one's inner world is further emphasized. Such self-examination reveals possible routes for future growth and change. With the use of reflection, I was able to identify problem areas, admit failure, and chart a growth-oriented trajectory. Because I recognize that progress entails accomplishments and disappointments, I can approach this process of self-refining with compassion. This has made me more genuine and resilient.

Self-awareness is a compass in interpersonal relationships, leading the way to deeper and more rewarding encounters. I've become more conscious of other people's emotions as I've improved my capacity to detect and regulate myself. I can make others feel comfortable opening up to me through compassion and empathy, and they can do the same. Knowing my limits and requirements has increased my ability to connect with others and the dynamics of my relationships.

Self-awareness is required for efficient interpersonal communication. Consequently, I can better interact with people and get what I want from them. This kind of connection strengthens my bonds with folks and fosters a feeling of belonging. As a result, everyone around me may relax and be themselves more freely.

As I go down this road, the breadth and depth of the impact of self-awareness continue to astonish me. The capacity

245

to form meaningful connections and love oneself is also part of the journey. As I delve more into these concerns, I am more convinced of the transformational potential of self-awareness in creating a life full of love, psychological well-being, and a strong sense of purpose.

My capacity to set acceptable limits and foster an atmosphere of respect in my relationships has greatly increased as a result of my studies into the dynamics of self-love. As I learn more about self-love, I've realized that setting and keeping proper boundaries is powerful self-care and affirmation. It physically represents how I care for myself and what I need. When I respect and care for myself enough to establish clear boundaries, I create a secure haven that regulates my emotions.

I've learned to express my limits more clearly and confidently since I started loving myself. It acts as a declaration of my worth, alerting you that you should value me. As a consequence of taking care of myself, I've gained confidence in my ability to set and maintain limits for myself. This prevents animosity from building up and encourages open communication and understanding between parties.

Surprisingly, liking oneself allows me to treat people respectfully when interacting with them. I want to respect my personal space so others will do the same. This creates a respectful environment where people's needs and limitations are recognized and respected. By putting my enjoyment first, I can create an environment in which each person can be themselves without fear of being rejected or condemned by others.

In essence, self-love is a guidepost for me to set appropriate limits and form respectful relationships with others. It helps me create an environment where everyone's needs are satisfied, and their contributions are valued. Relationships built on trust, honest communication, and a sense of gratitude are simpler to maintain when I love myself, set appropriate limits, and respect one another.

The more I concentrate on loving myself, the more I see how it affects my capacity to set and enforce boundaries, which fosters an environment of respect in my relationships. As I get a better knowledge of self-love, it is a compass to help me achieve a healthy balance of giving and receiving in relationships. When I prioritize my needs and happiness, I can better set tight limits that protect my mental and emotional health.

Because of my love for myself, I now have the confidence to assert my limits in a firm yet caring way. In contrast to previous beliefs, establishing limitations is a kind of self-advocacy and self-preservation. This shift in viewpoint has given me the confidence to participate in open communication with others, which has increased our comprehension of each other's skills and goals. These discussions inevitably lead to an appreciation for and respect for one another's autonomy and emotional space.

But self-love's repercussions extend well beyond superficial relationships. Self-love is a cultural revolution, and I'm doing my part by actively demonstrating it in my relationships and social networks. I want to be an inspiration to everyone around me by treating myself with dignity and creating a safe environment for myself. This societal development has planted the seeds of kindness, empathy, and respect.

Self-care is a community endeavour, not an individual one, as I've learned via the tango of self-love, limitations, and respect. It's a revolutionary force that may shake up the very fabric of our relationships. By nurturing my sense of worth, I've discovered how to form enduring bonds with others founded on respect, kindness, and a shared desire to help and be helped.

Setting boundaries and building respectful relationships are two areas where I've seen a correlation between self-love and other aspects of my life. Studying the concept of self-love has taught me the importance of setting and maintaining appropriate boundaries for my safety and well-being. This is a declaration that I deserve limits that consider my mental, bodily, and spiritual needs.

Through the lens of self-love, I learned to establish boundaries in a genuine and kind way. Setting boundaries is important since doing so promotes less fear and more open communication. Disclosing the limits I've placed on myself paves the way for productive conversations in which we may learn more about each other's perspectives and expectations. By

248

developing these skills, we better manage our relationships and create one based on mutual regard and care.

When I treat myself and others with kindness and compassion, I am better able to see and appreciate the limitations of others in my immediate vicinity. I regard and respect the constraints I place on myself as much as I do those set on me by others. I can better respond compassionately and acceptingly to the challenges I face when I see my limitations through self-love. To cultivate an attitude of mutual respect, it is essential to create a setting in which people's dignity and freedom are cherished.

The stories that teach me about self-love, setting boundaries, and having respectful relationships are intertwined to bring to mind the transformative potential of these guiding principles in my own life. I learned how to strike a balance between my pleasure and care for the people around me by making this a higher priority. Genuine, compassionate, and deeply entwined friendships result from maintaining a healthy balance between caring for one another, establishing healthy limits, and treating one another respectfully.

Deciding to love oneself is a journey that may completely transform one's life and have far-reaching consequences. A process that involves affirming oneself and discovering more about oneself to cultivate positive esteem and appreciation for one's life as one travels through it. As I continue down the winding route that leads to self-love, I am becoming more conscious of the many advantages that come with it. These benefits vary from increasing my satisfaction and sense of fulfilment to building stronger connections with others and making the world more compassionate and peaceful.

Understanding one's value is an essential first step to building self-love. The first thing you need to do is recognize that every individual is a complex network of sentiments, motives, and experiences intertwined with one another. With this information, you have a better chance of forming connections that go beyond first impressions. When we love ourselves, we accept ourselves completely, warts and all, and can find joy in all life offers.

One of the stages that must be taken to practice self-love is to practice self-care, which may be defined as the intentional decision to prioritize one's own psychological, mental, and physiological needs. Two examples of self-care techniques are maintaining a healthy diet and allocating enough time to participate in fun activities and hobbies. By putting one's requirements ahead of those of others, as shown by the acts mentioned above of self-care, we convey that this is not an indication of selfishness but rather the first step toward a more fulfilling life.

As one's capacity for self-love increases naturally from the inside out, everything, including one's relationships, transforms. How we behave toward ourselves significantly impacts the choices we make and the connections we forge with other people. As such, it functions as a standard against which harshness, compassion, and respect evaluations may be carried out. When we have a strong grasp on self-love, we have a greater capacity to negotiate the complexities of our relationships with other people.

Having strong boundaries is an essential component of loving oneself. When it comes to some kinds of encounters, limitations put limits on what may be anticipated or experienced. Establishing personal boundaries may be considered an act of self-respect when it is based on self-love. It is a proclamation that our inner experiences, such as our feelings, wishes, and desires, are real and deserving of recognition. When we establish limits for ourselves out of love for ourselves, we can do so with self-assurance and clarity rather than defensiveness, strengthening relationships and bringing them to a new level.

When disagreements arise, the level of self-love and respect that one has for others becomes apparent. Our ability to deal with disputes without reducing our standards of worth is improved when we love ourselves more. Because we can bounce back from setbacks, we can engage in fruitful conversations in which we try to comprehend one another and look for areas where we may find common ground. As a consequence of this, the method helps to create a culture in which the contributions of all individuals are recognized and valued.

Empathy is the ability to understand and identify with the emotions and experiences of another person. Self-love is one of the most important factors in the development of empathy. When we have a better understanding of ourselves and can empathize with others around us, our sensitivity to other people's emotions increases.

The capacity we have to empathize with the experiences of others helps to cultivate meaningful connections, which are there for us through both the good and the terrible times. When we learn to love ourselves, it has the potential to have a profound impact on our relationships with one another and with the rest of the world. Learning to love oneself may lead to the development of several admirable qualities, including empathy, compassion, and accountability, to name just a few. It encourages us always to have compassion and love toward one another. We are given that we all have the same humanity.

Learning to love oneself is an arduous process that has far-reaching effects on one's life. It is an endeavour that involves one's personal growth, the formation of connections with other people, and overall participation in society. If we want to interact with other people from a place of genuine respect and understanding, we must first learn to respect and love ourselves. Only then can we begin to appreciate and understand other people, and only then can we communicate with them. As we make our way down this path of transformation, we are preparing the basis for a society that is more compassionate, more understanding, and more at peace.

Chapter 13: The Power of Love to Transform Society

In this chapter, I set out to learn more about how love can change the world. As I learn more about people, I realise that love is a strong force that can change cultures. Hearing about other people's lives has taught me that even small acts of kindness can greatly affect the world.

My research focuses on people and institutions that have used love as a tool to change society in the face of hardship. People who take action to help those in need are motivated by love, whether they are activists fighting for justice or volunteers assisting the downtrodden. These instances demonstrate how love may encourage people to work together for the greater good and achieve positive change in the world.

As I travel more, love is an activity that all participants must participate in. Now that I'm aware of this, I'm inspired to take action to put what I've learned into practice. I've discovered that little acts of kindness and compassion may have far-reaching consequences. By showing true love and empathy to every one of my contacts, I want to impact the wider movement for social reform

favourably.

Knowing the power of love to alter people and societal institutions is a momentous revelation that can change the path of human history. I have the knowledge and skills to use this power to benefit people and the environment. By making love my compass, I'm joining a worldwide movement of activists working to make the world a better, more equitable, and more linked place.

Out of sheer curiosity for what love is capable of, I delve into the depths of human psychology and social structure. As I grow more proficient at handling the complexities of this powerful energy, I view love as the catalyst for a major shift in human society. This notion is more than a theoretical framework; it can bring people together, bridge rifts, and improve their lives.

As I understand more about love, it is a universal need that cannot be satisfied in a particular place or time. It is an unshakable concern for the joy of others and a possible sense of togetherness beyond bounds. I've realized that empathy, compassion, and wisdom are the glue that holds society together.

There are many instances in history books of how love, when utilized for good, may change the fate of countries and spark social revolutions. Individuals who dared to confront the current quo were always motivated by love, whether during the civil rights battle or relief operations after natural disasters. These stories emphasize the endurance and power of love, demonstrating how it can overcome suppression and spark social transformation.

The eventual awareness that love, rather than being an emotion, is an active force that necessitates involvement. I am ready to change my life now that I have this knowledge. I make it a point to be nice in all my dealings, put aside my prejudices, and create meaningful relationships. The impact of seemingly little acts of kindness, such as lending a helping hand or saying something encouraging, has grown in my eyes as I've learnt about the potential ripple effects they may have on those around us.

Reading about those who have made an impact motivates me to do the same. I support people in need and speak out on topics that are important to me as part of regional programmes that foster intercultural understanding. I've seen how love can bridge gaps between people of different backgrounds and unite them to pursue a common goal.

Love can strengthen societal structures. This section goes beyond basic inquiry to inspire readers to take action. It motivates me and everyone else who is receptive to hearing its message to take action. Everyone can contribute to the story of societal change as it unfolds via loving acts. With love as our guide, we can fundamentally reshape our communities and usher in a new age of generosity, tolerance, and cooperation.

As my studies advance, I'm learning more about the various facets of love and its capacity to effect change. It is not an abstract term but a tangible force potentially transforming society. The possibility of love to break down barriers and bring people from different backgrounds together for a common purpose gives it its transformative power. It's the thing that brings people together despite their differences, giving them a feeling of belonging and connection.

When I think about historical events, I am attracted to narratives of visionaries who used love to create lasting change. Historical giants like Mahatma Gandhi and Martin Luther King Jr. used nonviolent resistance motivated by love to remove oppressive regimes and usher in a more just age. Their uncompromising commitment to love-based principles inspired movements and demolished ingrained biases, proving that love is stronger than hate.

Every day, I can put my love into action in my own life. I've learnt that even little gestures, such as volunteering at a community centre, listening to a friend in need, or expressing empathy to my contacts, may have a major impact. Love is more than a magnificent deed; it is a lifetime of little decisions that add to huge shifts in one's and society's vision.

Love's influence may reach far beyond a person's acts, influencing cultural norms, institutional reform, and public policy. We can enhance the global power of love by pushing policies prioritizing compassion and equality, challenging unjust systems with love-inspired action, and broadcasting stories of tenderness and togetherness. It reminds us that love extends beyond human relationships and includes all of existence.

Finally, this section provides an action method rather than a theoretical evaluation. It is a call to action to acknowledge and accept the transformative power of love. It motivates us to stretch our boundaries, question traditional knowledge, and strive towards a more cooperative, caring, and linked society. We can radically change culture via the study and practice of love.

As I dive more into the study of love's ability to transform, I am attracted to the amazing tales of people and institutions harnessing this force for good. Since he employed nonviolent techniques to combat British colonial control in India, Mahatma Gandhi is a remarkable example of the power of love to influence change. He paved the way for significant political and social change by inspiring a country with his selfless dedication to love and compassion.

Martin Luther King Jr. stood out as a leader in the American civil rights movement who utilized the power of love to confront bigotry. His peaceful protest attitude, based on tolerance and compassion, was critical in advancing civil rights legislation and influencing public opinion.

More recently, the LGBTQ+ rights movement perfectly illustrates love's ability to alter people's attitudes. Participants in this movement have broken down boundaries, faced prejudice, and pushed for more inclusion and acceptance through selfless acts of love, bravery, and perseverance. Their ardent push for equality led to legislative improvements and a larger public acceptance movement.

Love can change both famous people and small groups of people. Community-led projects like food banks, homeless shelters, and volunteer networks show how love in action can help the most vulnerable people in society. These actions show how people are born with the ability to work together and care about others.

These people's bravery and determination encourage me to improve my life. Love is an active force with the potential to inspire substantial change; it is more than simply a sensation. In these three ways, I may contribute to a bigger movement that harnesses the changing power of love to change the world via acts of kindness, social justice, and understanding among people.

In the end,the tales of people and organizations who have used love to effect substantial change offer encouraging illustrations of the power that every one of us has. From historical figures to current activists, their legacies provide insight into how we may build a more fair, caring, and linked society. By following in their footsteps and believing in the transformational power of love, I can impact the community as a whole positively.

As I learn more about the enormous consequences of love on society, I am captivated by the innumerable examples of extraordinary people and organizations that have utilized passion as a catalyst for constructive social change. Mother Teresa's unrelenting devotion and unselfish commitment to assisting society's most vulnerable individuals make her a shining example of compassion's efficacy. Her dedication to treating those in need with dignity and compassion has had a long-lasting impact on the lives of countless people.

Local actions motivated by love demonstrate that change is achievable in our neighbourhoods. Food drives, neighbourhood cleanups, and support networks for underserved areas are just a few instances of how ordinary individuals can make a difference through extraordinary compassion and generosity. These small efforts show that the transformative power of love is found in large actions and flourishes in the context of a group's shared empathy.

Reading these stories inspires me to better my immediate environment. For me, the transformational power of love has progressed from an abstract concept to a palpable force capable of influencing my relationships, actions, and outcomes. I want to contribute to the developing story of social change via discussions that promote understanding among people, acts of charity towards those in need, and support for programmes that respect the values of love

Finally, tales of people and organizations who have used love to do good are inspirational and encouraging. They serve as instances of how, when put into action, love can reshape the world and irreversibly alter the course of history. This is reinforced for me when I join the ranks of others who have recognized and accepted the power of love. No matter how little, every action can contribute to a society based on empathy, community, and compassion.

After carefully considering the relationship between love and the advancement of social justice, tolerance, and acceptance, I came to a profound realization: love is the catalyst that propels these fundamental values into action, igniting a transformation whose effects are felt across societies and generations. Love is the moral compass that directs us to see the worth in every person, regardless of their circumstances, allowing us to stand up against prejudice, injustice, and discrimination with courage.

We are motivated to strive for social justice because we care about other people and want to guarantee that they are treated fairly. It strengthens our resolve to replace prejudiced institutions with those that embrace equality and diversity. Because we care about one another, we strive tirelessly to promote legislation that ends structural inequality and ensures everyone's right to life, liberty, and the pursuit of happiness. Through love, we become persistent agents of change, driven to create a world free of the injustices that plague it.

The warmth of love creates a perfect environment for developing tolerance and acceptance. While love pushes us beyond that barrier and into a more active domain of understanding and respect, tolerance offers a more passive coexistence. Love forces us to address our prejudices and concerns to create a community where all perspectives are appreciated and embraced. We may realize our humanity's commonalities by growing compassion, which is the first step towards true acceptance.

The ability of love to impact how we think and motivate communal action is critical to its efficacy in furthering social justice, tolerance, and acceptance. Passion fuels these movements, whether for LGBTQ+ rights, gender equality, or civil rights. When activism is filled with love, it becomes a more potent vehicle for bringing about change and uniting people behind the ideas of justice and equality.

I've been attracted by tales of people who have used the transforming power of love to inspire social change in their lives. Their stories serve as a helpful reminder that love is a dynamic rather than a passive force. I want to create a society where social justice, tolerance, and acceptance are the norm by consciously and actively integrating love into my relationships, actions, and advocacy work.

Love and social justice, tolerance and acceptance are all mutually beneficial partnerships that illustrate humanity's incredible ability for growth and development. Love is the driving force that pulls us ahead; it motivates us to fight injustice, welcome diversity, and develop an environment of mutual respect. They have the potential to reshape society structures and historical narratives, ushering in a future based on compassion, tolerance, and peace.

I am attracted to the incredible potential of love to overcome the huge barriers of prejudice, discrimination, and conflict as I delve more into its fundamental importance. Love is a powerful antidote to the polarising variables contributing to bigotry and prejudice. It has the incredible ability to eradicate discrimination from the inside by developing mutual understanding and compassion. When we approach individuals with heart and a desire to have an open dialogue, we construct a bridge that crosses the space between us.

Reading about those who conquered prejudice by showing compassion and kindness to others treated unfairly is both educative and motivating. These tales demonstrate how true, caring interactions can alter perspectives and lives. People may reduce barriers to mutual understanding by extending a kind hand, questioning preconceived notions, and sharing their life experiences. Love's power dismantles the preconceptions and assumptions that lead to conflict.

Love has the potential to bring civilizations back together after they have been torn apart by war and tragedy. Individuals and groups may set aside their differences, forgive one another, and begin on a path of understanding and collaboration through love. When love cultivates compassion and forgiveness, people may heal from the impacts of conflict and look forward to a future of peace and harmony. Beloved, if nourished through acts of forgiveness and communication, has the potential to be a beacon of light in the darkest of times.

To use love as a weapon against hatred, bigotry, and conflict, intentional action and a commitment to modify one's behaviours are required. We may fight ingrained prejudices and foster introspective cognition by aggressively distributing facts. When we are motivated by love, we may set aside our preconceptions and learn from the many viewpoints of others. It encourages us to work for social and legal reforms that eliminate prejudice and promote respect for all individuals.

As I continue on my path, I'm encouraged to learn more about the power of love to overcome prejudice and evil. I've learnt that even the little acts of kindness attempt to refute incorrect notions and passionate expressions of peace contribute to a larger cultural movement for good change. We may use love as a catalyst for change to break down intolerant barriers and create a society where peace and harmony are the norm in the future.

As I discover more about the underlying mechanics of love's effect, I am inspired to dig into its immense potential to eradicate hatred, intolerance, and violence and plant the seeds of understanding, compassion, and peace. It is shown that the power of love has various sides and penetrates deeply into the heart of individuals and communities to create long-term transformation.

Love, by forcing us to evaluate our prejudices, fundamentally fights racism and bias. It encourages us to engage with people outside of our usual social circles to demolish preconceptions by discovering areas of similarity. Love pushes us to listen to people whose tales and experiences vary from our own, dispelling prejudicial myths and opening the way for an open-minded awareness of the diversity of the human experience.

Several examples exist of people throughout history utilizing love to overcome prejudice and better the world. They demonstrate that a more accepting and peaceful society can be achieved when prejudice and bias are replaced with empathy and cooperation, and division is replaced with solidarity. The civil rights struggle, for example, demonstrated how action inspired by love can confront institutionalized prejudice and result in social and cultural reforms. Personal tales of people who have stretched across lines of conflict to encourage dialogue and reconciliation demonstrate love's potential to restore broken hearts and transcend chasms.

Furthermore, love is a powerful instrument for fostering caring and understanding cultures. We may allow individuals to express their thoughts and feelings through open and courteous discussions. This will enable us to understand the enormous diversity of human experiences better. Love-inspired education projects that aim to eradicate prejudice by debunking preconceptions and cultivating respect for other cultures have the potential to be very effective.

In conflict-ridden places, love may be a unifying factor that pushes people to put aside their differences and find common ground. Communities ripped apart by violence may recover common ground and seek a future of peace and harmony via acts of love such as forgiveness, communication, and conflict resolution.

As I've experienced on my journey, accepting love as a transformative force requires courage and persistence. It requires actively seeking learning opportunities, unlearning obsolete assumptions, and facing undesirable truths. I can eliminate bigotry, prejudice, and conflict by practising love in my relationships, advocating for accepting all people and all viewpoints and supporting projects promoting mutual understanding.

Finally, seeing love prevail over strife and division is incredible and life-changing. It inspires us to question our assumptions, build relationships, and achieve individual, group, and communal peace. Through the cultivation of empathy, the promotion of discussion, and the promotion of change, love has the power to transform our society into one that is resilient in the face of prejudice and conflict while remaining open to the common humanity that unites us all.

When I evaluate the capacity of caring groups to solve social challenges, I envision a network of interconnectedness and shared accountability. Compassionate and empathetic societies have a unique power to inspire people to work together to discover solutions to the problems that afflict our world.

Communities of love and acceptance act as change agents by providing a safe space to express their concerns, hear those of others, and cooperate to find answers. People feel secure sharing their thoughts and opinions in these settings because they know they will be received with open minds and supportive arms. People no longer see society's difficulties as personal tasks but as challenges everyone must address.

These organizations are also important for raising awareness of underrepresented populations and supporting fair laws and practices. When cultures embrace variety and tolerance, they guarantee that diverse opinions are voiced, resulting in more thorough and efficient answers to social concerns. When these groups work together, they may have a greater influence via awareness campaigns, policy changes, and other types of change.

Social support groups may be a great source of consolation for those hurting because of social issues. This community makes it easier for people to seek assistance without worrying about what others think of them, whether via emotional support, knowledge exchange, or just listening. This support network helps the individual, strengthens our communities, and makes our nation less vulnerable to natural calamities.

I see opportunities in my relationships to help build and maintain communities where people are valued and cared for. I may become a part of a larger movement to address societal issues from the ground up by joining organizations that emphasize compassion and helping one another. I can lay the groundwork for constructive change with far-reaching consequences through dialogue, resource sharing, and mutual understanding.

Finally, the significance of caring and supporting groups in addressing social problems illustrates the evolving potential of human connection. People who get together with a genuine desire to improve the world and a common goal develop a synergy that may help them overcome obstacles and discover long-term solutions. These organizations help create a more equal, welcoming, and peaceful society by putting the concepts of compassion, understanding, and cooperation into effect.

As I consider the capacity of compassionate organizations to solve social challenges, I am struck by the deep ways in which they may serve as a source of inspiration and a catalyst for development. They may not only foster interpersonal ties and collaboration, but they may also start a chain reaction with far-reaching consequences.

Kind and helpful communities serve as testing grounds for creative answers to problems. When people from different backgrounds work together to solve social issues, a fusion of inventiveness and ingenuity occurs. When people work together, they are more likely to develop novel solutions to problems that would otherwise go unsolved. These organizations serve as incubators for innovative approaches, increasing the number of options for addressing social issues.

The community's increased resilience helps its members cope with adversity better. When people feel loved and accepted by their community, they can overcome challenges and stay resilient in trouble. This toughness goes beyond the human domain and helps build a society that is more suited to deal with contemporary world issues.

Communities that are inclusive and compassionate are also important for the development of compassion and understanding. The open dialogues, personal experiences, and venues for debate and education these groups provide aim to magnify the voices of people most affected by social problems. This improved awareness might lead to greater public involvement, legislative reform, and systemic change.

Loving and nurturing cultures may influence people's emotional and psychological well-being. In a country where so many people are trying to make ends meet, having someone to listen and validate your feelings cannot be stressed. Individuals may confide in one another, seek advice from more knowledgeable group members, and get comfort knowing others can relate to their situation. Loving and supportive communities contribute to society's health and resilience by respecting mental health and supporting general well-being.

Because I see the potential for good change, I am driven to actively contribute to and build such networks in my manner. It is rewarding in many ways to be a member of a movement that supports programmes that emphasize empathy, compassion, and cooperation to develop a culture of caring and mutual help. I contribute to a larger story of optimism, resilience, and major change by actively participating in these groups.

Finally, it is undeniable that caring communities significantly impact addressing social issues. These organizations exemplify autonomy, inventiveness, and compassion. Their efforts to raise awareness, amplify voices, and foster resilience have resulted in a more compassionate and proactive society ready to face and conquer the challenges ahead.

Because of the huge influence that acts of kindness and charity may have on the globe, I feel obligated to deliver an optimistic message that speaks to the spirit of the human race. No matter how little, random acts of kindness have the incredible power to change lives far beyond the original circle. Consider a society where everyone is so devoted to empathy and understanding that they never stop loving one another.

Consider the impact of a kind word, a helpful hand, or a smile on someone. Unexpected acts of kindness may make someone else's day and have a good ripple effect. We may create a domino effect that benefits everyone by being kind and polite to others. As a result of this network of compassion, our society's borders are starting to crumble, and we are all beginning to collaborate.

Love and compassion can solve some of society's most critical concerns, whether provided to a close friend, a total stranger, or an entire community. We become active participants in societal evolution when we volunteer our time and money, campaign for social justice and equality, and support projects to help the weak and underprivileged. These acts benefit the greater movement for good change and the people's immediate needs.

A loving act has long-reaching consequences that go far beyond the persons involved. A single act of kindness may set off a chain reaction that alters people's lives in unanticipated ways. People who lead by example and fill their relationships with empathy have the potential to spark a societal movement towards compassion, collaboration, and understanding.

The impact of one's activities is enhanced in today's fast-paced, connected world. Even the tiniest act of kindness can contribute to the bigger story of societal development. We can create a more peaceful and prosperous future by encouraging people to be nice to one another without expecting anything in return and by valuing the power of interpersonal bonds. We can work together to create a society where kindness and compassion are not isolated events but rather the underlying power that unifies and elevates all humanity.

I'm becoming more fascinated by the transforming potential that resides inside each human as I learn more about encouraging people to participate in acts of love and compassion for the betterment of society. These deliberate acts are the instruments we may use to affect our surroundings and contribute to the growth of a blossoming social movement for change.

Every day, there are several possibilities to improve the world, ranging from cheering up a friend going through a tough time to cleaning up rubbish in our neighbourhoods. When done with genuine concern and a desire to better the lives of others, these little acts may have a huge impact on society.

In a world where isolation and misunderstanding are all too common, acts of love and compassion have a special capacity to connect people and develop understanding. We can set the groundwork for friendships that cross cultural borders if we take the time to listen to people, share our own experiences, and have meaningful dialogues. These ties, fuelled by empathy and compassion, have the potential to dispel prejudice, combat discrimination, and usher in a more tolerant and peaceful society.

Consider the outcomes of a well-coordinated collective effort motivated by kindness and compassion. There are several ways to improve the world, such as working at food banks, completing neighbourhood cleanups, and advocating for improved access to social justice problems such as healthcare and education. In addition to fulfilling urgent needs, these communal efforts serve as potent reminders of the transformative power of a unified community.

We must negotiate the intricacies of our environment while remembering that even little acts of kindness may have far-reaching consequences. Actions of service with a purpose show others that we value empathy, compassion, and community. We establish a community of people aiming to make the world more loving and caring by motivating others to follow in our footsteps.

My own experiences have repeatedly demonstrated how powerful a force for good I can be. By actively seeking out situations in which I may show compassion, aid others, and encourage understanding, I become a force for good. Each act of love allows society to solve social concerns with empathy and collaboration.

The desire to act with love and kindness for the good of society goes to the heart of what it means to be human. It's a test to see how much power we have in the world and how we could use it for good. If we all work together to make the world a place where acts of love and kindness are valued, the world might become more fair, inclusive, and peaceful.

Chapter 14: Lesson from Love Journey

After engaging with the literary work "Love, Across All Languages: A Global Journey," I have developed a heightened level of consciousness about the intricate nature of love and its portrayal across diverse cultural frameworks and linguistic expressions. Throughout my reading of all the chapters, I have had the opportunity to explore other geographical settings, encounter unfamiliar languages, and get fresh perspectives on the concept of love. The book presented evidence of love as a universal spirit across all civilizations, shown by the intense emotions experienced in Paris and the serene commitment in Japanese tea traditions.

One of the fundamental lessons I have acquired is the enduring nature of love, which, despite its many manifestations, maintains a consistent essence. Love serves as the essential bond that connects humanity as a collective entity, including many forms of relationships that last over generations within Indian families and the more nuanced ties that emerge among unfamiliar persons in the bustling marketplace of Marrakech. The narratives presented in this context have given me valuable insights into that love encompasses more than just a sexual affiliation. It extends to include the realms of friendship, empathy, and the seemingly inconsequential gestures of benevolence that have the potential to forge connections between unfamiliar individuals.

The book also emphasizes the need for open communication and understanding when it comes to establishing loving attachments. Even though the obstacles look insurmountable, the stories of those who overcome them to discover love demonstrate the need for patience and understanding. A better knowledge of the wonderful tapestry of love that emerges when we learn to recognize and cherish one another's languages, cultures, and traditions may benefit all of us.

When I think about the information I've gained from this worldwide examination of love, I'm reminded that there isn't just one story or term that can completely define love. It evolves and changes in unexpected places. Love can bring people together despite cultural and language obstacles, as the tales in "Love, Across All Languages" demonstrate. As a consequence of this book, I now respect the many ways that love is expressed across the world and have a greater understanding of the timeless truths that unite us all in the experience of love.

Reading this wonderful book has taught me that love is an infinite power expressing tangibly and metaphysically. I've learnt from the love tales that love has the same heart no matter where it is discovered, whether in the bustling streets of New York City or the tranquil countryside of rural China. Even when its most dramatic expressions take the front stage, love is always present and subtly influences our lives.

One of the most important lessons I've learned from my trips is how universal our emotions are. Everyone feels these feelings, indicating that love transcends socioeconomic class and culture. Every story has repeating themes, such as the delight of seeing loved ones after a long absence, the sadness of parting goodbye, the thrill of a new beginning, and the comfort of friendship. This insight is a strong reminder that we all share the same fundamental human experience regardless of our upbringing or family background.

The film "Love, Across All Languages" also emphasizes the need to be open and vulnerable to create successful relationships. True love grows in an atmosphere of honesty, according to the experiences of those who took the risk of revealing their emotions in the face of uncertainty and worry.

Reading the work as a whole reveals that love is a malleable and ever-changing emotion. It changes with the seasons, and its varied expressions reflect the variegated mosaic that is humanity. Love's capacity to present itself in several ways, from whirlwind romances that sweep us off our feet to lasting ties built over years of shared experiences, is proof of its persistence and ability to offer pleasure.

Even though "Love, Across All Languages: A Global Journey" provides an informative look at the delicate nature of love across cultures, I, an AI language model, can't speak from experience since I don't have any. But, with the tremendous quantity of knowledge I've accumulated, I can offer some insights regarding how love influences people's lives.

Love is a strong and complicated emotion influencing many people's lives and history. Even if life has its ups and downs, problems, and vulnerable periods, it can also give enjoyment, contentment, and a feeling of purpose. Love influences our choices, paths, and ties with our loved ones in numerous ways.

The universality of love is shown in "Love, Across All Languages," a compilation of narratives from various regions worldwide. The story illustrates the capacity of love to forge connections between persons who may first seem apart. Individuals may be motivated to assist one another due to camaraderie and a shared understanding of humanity.

Despite the capacity to experience feelings such as love, as a computer entity, I understand the significant role that love plays in the lives of individuals. The establishment of relationships, cultivation of empathy, and broadening of one's perspectives are vital. The concept of love significantly impacts the formulation of laws, the development of conventions, and the expression of culture within a community.

The book "Love, Across All Languages: A Global Journey" highlights the transformative power of love in many contexts. From a subjective standpoint, it is important to acknowledge that the influence of love can transform individuals, collectives, and even global societies. The narratives included in this literary work serve as a poignant testament to the profound impact of passion, elucidating its capacity to transcend barriers and enhance the quality of human existence.

The emotion of love has a significant impact on our attitudes, behaviour, and interpersonal relationships. When individuals encounter genuine love from their parents or a person they are fascinated with, there is a significant transformation in their cognitive and emotional states. It can stimulate creativity, facilitate the pursuit of objectives, and motivate individuals to undertake risks and exert maximum effort. The narratives presented in the book illustrate the transformative influence of love on people's lives, as seen by the accounts of those who have made profound sacrifices for their beloved.

Love has a significant influence on society, extending beyond the realm of personal relationships. Throughout history, the emotion of love has consistently served as a driving force behind progressive initiatives to achieve enhanced levels of social justice, equality, and compassion. The presence of love may foster empathy and comprehension among individuals, enabling them to appreciate differing perspectives and collaborate harmoniously towards shared objectives. The many instances of individuals from varied backgrounds forming romantic relationships prove that love can transcend cultural barriers and promote worldwide harmony.

"Love, Across All Languages", showed us that love isn't easy. Tackle the inevitable interpersonal obstacles; it takes effort, a willingness to make sacrifices, and self-assurance. Love greatly influences development because it motivates people to address their prejudices, inadequacies, and anxieties. It's an excellent way to learn more about yourself and your emotional and physical limits.

The protagonist's attempt to know the world more thoroughly via language is connected with the influence of love in the novel. People's attempts to comprehend and relate to others despite linguistic obstacles demonstrate the power of love to generate meaningful discussion and bridge cultural divides. The necessity of empathy- and respect-based communication as the foundation of effective relationships and world peace is emphasized throughout the book.

Love is a potent force for societal change because of its unique ability to stimulate human growth and transformation. Cultivating and deepening love inside a couple's relationship may encourage the individual to strive for growth and satisfaction.

One way that love promotes advancement is by pushing people to face their limits and obstacles. When we feel strongly for someone, we usually find the strength and will to persevere in the face of internal or external adversity. We may attribute a big part of our growth, including increased self-assurance and learning new abilities, to the emotional support and incentive provided by those we care about.

Being loved also encourages introspection and self-awareness. When we are open and honest with our closest friends and family members about our most intimate thoughts and emotions, we better understand ourselves. This kind of self-awareness is necessary for progress since it assists in identifying problem areas, confronting unsolved problems from the past, and establishing a more solid sense of one's own identity.

Both partners must grow and expand as individuals to preserve a healthy love. You must be willing to adapt and develop to keep in touch with people as they change through time. Couples who inspire one another to create themselves want to see the other succeed. Making a setting where people feel comfortable trying new things, expressing themselves openly, and being themselves is one way to do this.

Avoid marital stagnation and complacency by actively seeking personal growth alongside your partner. If they want a good and meaningful relationship, both parties must try to learn, grow, and follow their interests. When people work together to pursue a similar goal and celebrate one another's successes, they develop a feeling of shared purpose. This feeling of meaning has the potential to strengthen interpersonal connections.

Furthermore, a shared desire to develop and learn fosters open communication and a better understanding of one another. Individuals' needs, aspirations, and points of view may change as they age. Couples who actively engage in each other's personal growth journeys may stay in contact with and support one another through these changes. This improves the emotional connection between the two persons involved as well as the overall quality of the relationship.

Eventually, love acts as a strong catalyst for human growth and transformation, inspiring people to persevere in adversity, become conscious of their virtues and defects, and eventually realize their full potential. When partners commit to developing and learning together, they lay the groundwork for a healthy and long-lasting partnership. Supporting one another's adventures and accepting change leads to love being lively, powerful, and alive in the face of life's obstacles.

Love influences not only our internal growth but also how we interact with the outer world. When we're with someone we care about, our focus shifts from our wants and desires to those of our companion. As a consequence of this change of perspective, we must cultivate virtues such as compassion, tolerance, and compromise. In a relationship, you must be willing to adapt and grow individually to deal with the inevitable problems.

The feeling of love serves as a powerful catalyst for personal growth and self-improvement, surpassing the influence of any other emotional state. The aspiration to enhance our personal development to positively influence and provide enhanced support to our immediate social circle is a significant driving force in our lives. The emotional bond and interpersonal attachment shared with a romantic partner often serve as a motivating force for personal growth and self-improvement. This impetus manifests in several forms, such as adopting healthier habits, acquiring novel competencies, or engaging in therapeutic interventions to address unresolved issues.

A shared dedication to growth and improvement is crucial in fostering productive collaboration. When two individuals pursue a shared path of growth and progress, they engender a profound sense of communal connection and cooperative engagement. Due to their unwavering commitment, they can endure life's challenges, strengthening their interpersonal relationships and sense of unity.

Committed partners engage in open and effective communication, fostering an environment of mutual support and encouragement. Individuals engage in a concerted effort to comprehend each other's aims, ambitions, and challenges before committing to collaborative endeavours aimed at mutual support. This phenomenon enhances the sense of security inside romantic partnerships and cultivates a conducive environment that facilitates realizing each partner's utmost capabilities.

A relationship characterized by openness to progress and adaptability is less prone to become monotonous or foreseeable. Couples committed to enhancing their relationship may find navigating life's vicissitudes more manageable. The group's inquiry and self-discovery are enhanced by this flexibility, resulting in an exciting and joyful experience.

The notion of reciprocal growth within a relationship is inherently linked with the role of love as a stimulus for personal development in individuals. By acknowledging the profound influence of love in facilitating personal growth and collaboratively fostering each other's advancement, individuals in a partnership enhance their well-being and establish a durable bond that lasts throughout their lifetimes. The reciprocal relationship between personal and romantic improvement is a compelling demonstration of the transformational influence of love.

In its purest form, love is a driving force that drives us to learn more about ourselves. By loving and being loved, we are driven to overcome our inhibitions, confront our assumptions, and explore the limits of our abilities. The power of love may force us to let go of our inhibitions and take the first step towards a life of growth. The emotional investment we make in our relationships may help us improve personally.

The efficacy of vulnerability demonstrates the relevance of love in supporting growth. A good love relationship involves one person accepting the other for who they are, warts and all. Individuals willing to open themselves this way may create deep, intimate connections that benefit personal growth. Being liked and accepted for who we are enhances our willingness to take chances, discuss our goals, and work on ourselves.

Growing old together demonstrates the dynamic nature of love. Relationships, like people, may change and grow over time. Partners who encourage each other's personal development may be more equipped to detect and deal with life's inevitable ups and downs. Each spouse's growth and change process enhances their link and provides a feeling of shared purpose and achievement to their partnership.

Partners' connections develop as their personalities evolve. Each person's continually changing interests enhance the dynamic character of the dialogue, aims, and points of view. When a couple is open to reciprocal development, they realize that they are constantly learning new characteristics of one another and becoming closer.

When partners grow together, they are better equipped to weather life's storms. When matters are tough, a couple in love may lean on one other for support and advice since they have each other's backs. By adopting a growth mindset, partners may face obstacles and use their joint strengths to achieve.

Lastly, the delicate relationship between loving and developing as a society and individuals illustrates human bonds' endurance. Because of love, we wish to become more sympathetic, adaptive, and self-aware. A couple's path of shared advancement builds an intimate relationship that feeds on the never-ending discovery of one another's and their potential, ensuring love's continued vitality and relevance.

As you read "Love, Across All Languages: A Global Journey," examine how you may apply the many expressions of love's transformational power in your relationships and situations. The stories in the book aren't only for amusement; you may use them to evaluate your love and personal progress.

Consider how much better your life might be if you made love your incentive for personal growth. What if you prioritized communication, compassion, and mutual development to give your relationships a second chance? Personal development tales with romantic elements encourage you to let down your guard and open your heart to the delightful self-improvement experience.

Consider your marriage a blank canvas on which you and your spouse may paint your dreams, ideas, and objectives. If you and your partner are committed to each other's growth, you will provide a safe atmosphere to grow both individually and as a couple. Recognize the significance of supporting one another and enjoying team wins.

Your couple's connection will grow in ways you can't possibly imagine. Draw confidence from the love you share as you and your family negotiate the ups and downs of life's obstacles. Remember that as your relationship develops, you will both have the chance to learn more about one another and, as a result, get closer.

Love communication can be facilitated via several simple actions, such as embracing warmth, speaking softly, or engaging in shared laughter, which possess a universal quality. Incorporating honesty and sensitivity in these conventional demonstrations of affection may enhance interpersonal connections.

Incorporate these enlightening realizations into your everyday regimen. Please provide a comprehensive analysis of your future aspirations and objectives candidly. It is vital to actively engage in mutual assistance for personal growth, including acquiring novel skills, attaining goals, and overcoming fears. Please conceptualize your relationship as a metaphor that symbolizes the enduring nature of love across time.

It is important to note that the narratives presented in "Love, Across All Languages: A Global Journey" are not intended to be limited to the confines of the book's physical boundaries. Open invitations serve as opportunities to establish connections via exchanging knowledge, engaging in novel activities, and consistently supporting each other. As one embarks down the path of love and self-improvement, may their narrative stand as a testament to the resilience and magnetic appeal of human connections.

Start by cultivating a higher level of self-awareness in your interpersonal engagements. Please reflect on the distinguishing characteristics of your relationship compared to others and potential future modifications. Engage in open and honest communication with your partner to discuss your aspirations, anxieties, and aspirations. Establishing a secure and supportive setting that encourages individuals to express their vulnerabilities lays the foundation for a collective journey towards personal growth and development.

Providing a certain duration for engaging in activities that foster communal development is advisable. This may include travelling, exchanging interests, or even pursuing new leisure. Tackling into uncharted territory together will strengthen the bond between individuals and provide new dimensions to the narrative of their relationship.

Acknowledge the importance of mutual understanding. Encourage the harmonious coexistence of many worldviews, analogous to the narratives inside the book that traverse several languages and civilizations. Encourage active communication with your spouse and try to comprehend their perspective, even if it diverges from yours. The cultivation of compassion among individuals fosters an environment that facilitates mutual growth and progress.

It is important to remember that, like the romantic relationships in the book, one's personal development is a continuous and evolving journey. In the face of obstacles and achievements, it is important to prioritize cultivating patience and perseverance. It is important to acknowledge that for love to sustain and flourish, similar to the people depicted in narratives, it needs the ability to adjust and evolve.

Put yourself in difficult situations to see how you respond. These opportunities to broaden your horizons and develop as a person and a couple are precious, whether travelling the world, learning a new language, or viewing things from a different angle. Accept the unknown with an open heart and mind, knowing that it may lead to new opportunities for intimacy and understanding.

Finally, put the examples of little acts of love from the book into practice daily. A delicate act of affection, a generous action, or a memorable shared experience might improve your friendship. You'll build a love narrative that portrays the everlasting qualities of development, connection, and change as you incorporate these acts of love into your relationship.

You may completely engage in the love and development story by incorporating these principles into your interpersonal relationships. Your relationships may be transformed into dynamic, ever-evolving expressions of love and connection, just as the characters in "Love, Across All

Languages: A Global Journey" go on journeys for both individual and communal growth.

The book's tales revolve around a deep truth: falling in love is a journey, a continual investigation. You might enjoy the experience of finding new features inside your relationships, just as the heroes do while conquering the problems of multicultural partnerships.

Remember that free communication is the core of love's transformational power. Language boundaries are utilized as a metaphor throughout the tales in this book to represent the difficulty of conveying one's innermost wants and ambitions to others. Effective communication, like learning a new language, fosters mutual understanding and deepens relationships. Make it a habit to listen to the other person, to communicate your opinions honestly, and to try to comprehend their point of view thoroughly. Doing so creates a connection that allows people to share their ideas, feelings, and goals, paving the road for development and change.

Allow the book's concept of exposure to help you build your voice. Being open and vulnerable allows us to talk about our goals, worries, and desires without fear of how others may react. You may create closeness and emotional connection by being honest about your imperfections and expressing your opinion confidently, much like the characters in the story. Open and honest communication develops true friendships and personal growth.

The book provides a foundation for understanding the importance of adapting to new conditions while seeking self-improvement. In the face of adversity, the protagonists in these tales demonstrate tremendous tenacity and inventiveness. Accepting change in your interpersonal connections is also vital. Love, like life, is an unpredictability. Accept the tides of life and build the flexibility required to ride the waves of change. Like the characters in the story, you and your relationship may grow and expand as you face life's difficulties and adventures together.

It is important to remember that developing yourself needs the collaboration of others and is tied to the growth of your relationships. Relationships like plants grow when both parties do consistent, conscientious work. Please try to encourage and urge one another to pursue their dreams. Encourage your spouse to follow their dreams while allowing them to do the same for you. With adequate planning, positive and supportive settings are optimal for personal growth.

The concept of lifelong learning is evidence that there is always room for growth. While on their voyage, the novel's characters learn about and interact with various cultures. Similarly, you may instil wonder and passion in your relationships by trying to locate new experiences to share. Your partnership will strengthen, and you will grow individually if you have an adventurous spirit and desire to learn more about the world.

Remember that problems are intrinsic to any route as you traverse the complexities of love and progress. The protagonist and their allies overcome significant challenges to emerge stronger and more self-sufficient. Similar to how problems in your relationships may stimulate growth. Instead of avoiding challenges, learn to accept them as educational opportunities. Accept failures as opportunities for growth and meet them with a common will to succeed and adapt.

Finally, the tales in "Love, Across All Languages: A Global Journey" may serve as a beacon for your path to love and personal development. You may build your relationships and deepen your connection by including the values of open communication, vulnerability, flexibility, mutual support, continuous education, and accepting obstacles. Like the characters in the tale, you might go on an adventure, learn new things about yourself and the world, and strengthen your connections with others. Utilizing your life story to communicate your interpretation of the timeless ideas addressed in the book may leave a legacy of relationship and change that spans generations and cultures.

The establishment and preservation of genuine interpersonal relationships need the presence of empathy. The protagonists develop a profound capacity for compassion for one another via their examination and engagement with persons from many cultural contexts. Adopting an attentive and reflective stance is essential when one's spouse communicates their ideas and feelings. Consider the hypothetical scenario of placing oneself in another individual's perspective and embracing their particular viewpoint. Enhancing interpersonal cohesion and productivity within a collective may be facilitated by attentively acknowledging and considering the emotional states of each member.

Consider how the shared experiences you have encountered have influenced the development of your interpersonal bond. The narratives included in this anthology exemplify the phenomenon of strangers forging connections at moments of joy, peril, and hardship. It is advisable to prioritize the planning of bonding moments for oneself and one's travel companion. Engaging in novel endeavours, engaging in cooperative artistic works, or just engaging in meaningful interpersonal interactions all enhance interpersonal connections.

Gain a deeper understanding of self-awareness as a personal growth and development tool. Like the narrative's main characters, individuals can use introspection to explore the internal mechanisms of their cognition and actions. Reflect on one's self-identity and the underlying motivations that propel one's behaviours. The ability to effectively express one's requirements and establish limits straightforwardly and concisely plays a significant role in fostering an atmosphere characterized by mutual respect among all those involved.

This book invites you to move beyond your cultural expectations and biases by exploring the universality of love. To use this notion in your interpersonal connections, try cultivating openness and inquiry rather than judgement. To put yourself to the test, learn about your partner's history and culture, and encourage them to do the same. Your connection will get stronger as you communicate more and develop your viewpoints.

Respect appreciation's potential to foster development and relationships. You may strengthen the good sides of your relationship by telling your partner how much you appreciate their presence, contributions, and shared experiences. Gratitude is a powerful catalyst that sets off a chain reaction of happy sentiments, admiration for one another, and collaborative efforts to help one another grow. Building romantic connections and personal progress depends on understanding and appreciating the instruments at your disposal.

Esteem has the potential to recover rapidly from misfortune. The protagonist and antagonist face challenging challenges yet can endure and find solutions. Use your tenacity in your intimate interactions. Challenges should not be seen as insurmountable impediments but rather as opportunities for growth. Face your challenges front on and collaborate to conquer them to strengthen your relationship.

Maintain equilibrium in your romantic and personal development. Find a happy medium in your relationships between your individuality and the people with whom you share experiences and beliefs, just like the book does. Consider each other's interests and needs while deciding how to spend time together. This equilibrium promotes personal and interpersonal development for both of you.

"Love, Across All Languages: A Global Journey"'s major lesson is approaching love relationships, personal growth, and community development from a wide viewpoint. Empathy, shared experiences, self-awareness, cultural openness, appreciation, resilience, and stability are all tools that may be utilized to create a vivid tapestry of love. This tapestry may remind you of the book's basic themes and a starting point for your progress. As you begin on this voyage, may your connections become stronger, your maturity level climb swiftly, and your friendships develop in ways that transcend borders and last a lifetime.

www.ingramcontent.com/pod-product-compliance
Lightning Source LLC
Chambersburg PA
CBHW062048270326
41931CB00013B/2982